LIBRARY *of* GREAT AUTHORS

The

LIBRARY *of*
GREAT AUTHORS
series explores the
intimate connection between
writing and experience, shedding light
on the work of literature's most esteemed
authors by examining their lives. The
complete LIBRARY *of* GREAT AUTHORS brings
an excitingly diverse crowd to your bookshelf:

Albert Camus
Lewis Carroll
Fyodor Dostoevsky
Barbara Kingsolver
Gabriel García Márquez
Toni Morrison
Vladimir Nabokov
J.K. Rowling
J.R.R. Tolkien
Virginia Woolf

❧

Each book in the LIBRARY *of* GREAT AUTHORS
features full-length analysis of the writer's
most famous works, including such novels as
*Crime and Punishment, Lolita, The Lord of
the Rings,* and *Mrs. Dalloway.* Whether you
are a reader craving deeper knowledge of
your favorite author, a student studying the
classics, or a new convert to a celebrated
novel, turn to the LIBRARY *of* GREAT AUTHORS
for thorough, fascinating, and insightful
coverage of literature's best writers.

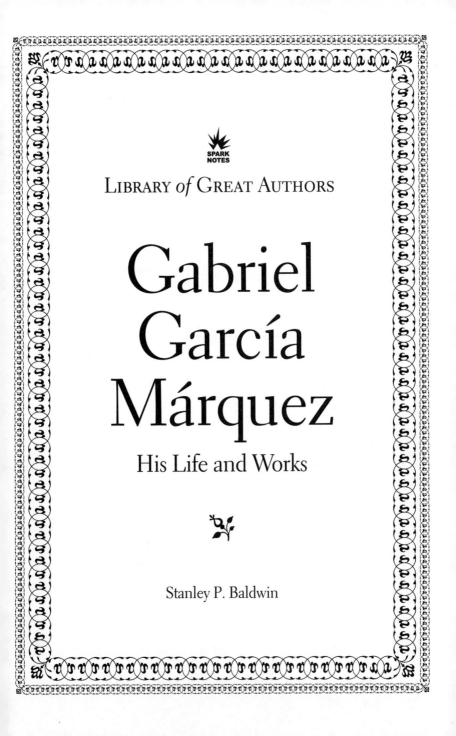

SPARK NOTES

LIBRARY *of* GREAT AUTHORS

Gabriel García Márquez

His Life and Works

Stanley P. Baldwin

EDITORIAL DIRECTOR Justin Kestler
EXECUTIVE EDITOR Ben Florman
SERIES EDITOR Emma Chastain

INTERIOR DESIGN Dan Williams

Produced by The Wonderland Press and published by SparkNotes

Spark Publishing
A Division of SparkNotes LLC
120 5th Avenue
New York, NY 10011

Any book purchased without a cover is stolen property, reported as "unsold and destroyed" to the Publisher, who receives no payment for such "stripped books."

10 9 8 7 6 5 4 3 2 1

Please submit comments or questions, or report errors to www.sparknotes.com/errors

Printed and bound in the United States of America

ISBN 1-58663-837-8

Library of Congress Cataloging-in-Publication Data available on request

Contents

Contents

III.
{ Chronicle of a Death Foretold }
53

IV.
{ Love in the Time of Cholera }
87

Contents

❧

{ Topics In Depth }

LIBRARY *of* GREAT AUTHORS

Gabriel García Márquez

I

THE LIFE OF GABRIEL GARCÍA MÁRQUEZ

Gabriel José García Márquez, Nobel Prize–winning author and longtime journalist, was born on March 6, 1928. His birthplace was Aracataca, a small banana town near the Caribbean coast in northern Colombia, South America. His mother, **Luisa Santiaga Márquez Iguarán,** came from a political family. His maternal grandfather, **Colonel Nicolás Ricardo Márquez Mejía**, was a Liberal veteran of the War of a Thousand Days, one of the many civil wars between Liberals and Conservatives that bloodied Columbia.

Luisa Santiaga Márquez fell in love with **Gabriel Eligio García,** a former medical student and a newcomer to the town. Not only was García a Conservative, he was reputedly a womanizer who had already fathered four illegitimate children, and Colonel Mejía did not think him a suitable match for his beloved daughter. However, no one counted on the persistence and imagination of Gabriel García. Daily, García sent Luisa Santiaga Márquez letters, packets of poems, and telegrams. He also sang original love ballads beneath her window.

Eventually, the family of Luisa Santiaga Márquez succumbed to Gabriel García's demonstrations of love and allowed Luisa to marry her stubborn suitor. The newlyweds had a rocky start. Aracataca's profitable banana boom ended in 1928 when the town was hit hard by a strike and suffered in its bitter aftermath. During one night alone, more than one hundred strikers were shot dead and dumped in a common grave. Making money became difficult for Gabriel García, especially after the birth of a baby, Gabriel García Márquez, nicknamed **Gabo** or **Gabito**. The couple found paying their bills almost impossible.

Eventually, Luisa and Gabriel relinquished their son to the care of his grandparents. He was reared in a mostly female household, surrounded by his maternal grandmother and numerous aunts. García Márquez has said that living in this environment was one of the best things that happened to him, since it inspired much of his future work. His superstitious aunts filled his mind with spine-tingling tales of magic and ghosts, while his grandfather told stories of the civil war and the banana massacre. García Márquez has often credited these relatives with his gifts for storytelling, in particular for his unique brand of magical realism.

When García Márquez was twelve, the family sent him to a Jesuit school about thirty miles north of Bogotá. Upon graduation, he entered the National University of Colombia to study law. During the next few years, while studying law, he began writing short stories, publishing eleven of them in *El Espectador*. García Márquez experienced a literary epiphany when he read the short story "The Metamorphosis" by **Franz Kafka** (1883–1924). García Márquez suddenly realized that he could write like Kafka, for in Kafka's story, he heard the voice of his grandmother. Stylistically, García Márquez's first stories reflect his fondness for the novels of American author **William Faulkner** (1897–1962). They use Faulkner's stream-of-consciousness technique and ability to present shifting points of view.

> " I was a 28-year-old newspaper-man with a published novel and a literary prize in Colombia, but I was adrift and without direction in Paris."
>
> **GABRIEL GARCÍA MÁRQUEZ**

García Márquez became bored with the study of law. Life in Bogotá might have become oppressive had he not met a beautiful thirteen-year-old Egyptian girl, **Mercedes Barcha Pardo**. He found her the most fascinating person he had ever talked with, so he proposed. She told him that they would have to wait to be married, but she swore a vow of love and fidelity to him. Fourteen years later, they were married.

García Márquez welcomed the opportunity to move to Cartagena when political violence closed Bogatá's National University, because he had realized that his studies in law school had little to do with seeing justice done in human rights cases. In Cartagena, he began working as a journalist, and in the years to come, he would write for many more newspapers. He also published two short stories, one of which won a prestigious Bogatá literary prize.

In 1954, García Márquez worked as a news correspondent from the Vatican, in Rome, and he published the novel *Leaf Storm* to glowing reviews. Critics hailed *Leaf Storm* as one of the finest novels ever written by a Colombian author. The following year, García Márquez moved to Paris and began writing full time. In the beginning, he wrote to stave off panic. He had very little money, no work permit, and only a little knowledge of French, so for three years he stayed in his hotel room and wrote. Eventually, he published his widely praised novel *No One Writes to the Colonel* (1956), the story of an old colonel who is near death and materially impoverished, but who fiercely clings to life and dignity. In an interview, García Márquez said that he wrote and rewrote the novel eleven times.

These impoverished, nerve-racking three years in Paris were García Márquez's crucible. After passing through this crucible, he realized that writing was his true vocation. He had both the talent and the self-discipline to write.

García Márquez returned to Colombia and married Mercedes, the girl to whom he had proposed long before. She had waited for him, just as in *Love in the Time of Cholera* (1985) Florentino Ariza waits many years for Fermina Daza. Missing the intensity of being a journalist, and sympathizing with the Castro revolution in Cuba, García Márquez cofounded a Bogotá branch of Castro's *Prensa Latina* news agency. In 1959, he spent time in both New York City and Cuba. His stay in the U.S. was not pleasant. New York overwhelmed him with its tangle of Kafkaesque red tape about the legitimacy of his visa. Relieved to leave the city, García Márquez boarded a bus for Mexico, looking forward to touring Faulkner's Deep South. On the way there, however, he was forced to endure demeaning, insulting racism because of his dark skin.

In addition to working as a journalist, in Mexico City García Márquez penned movie scripts and began writing a long novel, *In Evil Hour*, published in Spain in 1962 after undergoing heavy revision at the hand of its publisher. The novel won a Colombian literary contest. *Big Mama's Funeral*, a collection of short stories, was also published in 1962, and three years

> "*One Hundred Years of Solitude* is a thrilling piece of work, the apogee of the Latin-American literary renaissance in novels . . . I'd rather have seen Borges get it; he's at the end of his career. Márquez is a writer of true significance, yet offhand, I can't think of anyone who has received the Nobel who has published less."
>
> **JOHN UPDIKE**

later, in 1965, García Márquez began his masterpiece, *One Hundred Years of Solitude*. He has said that when he told Mercedes he was going to write, he said, "don't bother me, especially don't bother me about money." A year and a half later, he emerged from his study and announced that he was finished. "Good," Mercedes reportedly replied, "we owe twelve thousand dollars."

One Hundred Years of Solitude won almost every literary prize awarded in the Western world, including the French *Prix du Meilleur Livre Etranger* and the Italian *Primo Chianciano*. American critics declared it peerless, and the novel won Venezuela's Rómulo Gallegos Prize, as well as the Books Abroad/Neustadt International Prize in Literature. A decade later, García Márquez was awarded the Nobel Prize for Literature in Stockholm.

Since the publication of *One Hundred Years of Solitude*, García Márquez has continued to receive accolades for his novels, especially *Chronicle of a Death Foretold* (1981) and *Love in the Time of Cholera* (1985). Today, he lives in Mexico City and, despite being diagnosed with lymphatic cancer, has begun a projected three-volume set of memoirs.

Gabriel García Márquez

🌿

Events and Trends

That Influenced García Márquez's Work

Political Unrest in Colombia: When García Márquez published *One Hundred Years of Solitude* in 1967, populist factions in Colombia were still battling Conservative forces after more than a hundred years of civil war. Guerrilla groups established headquarters in the mountains, labor strikes continued, and assassinations sabotaged attempts at unity. In time, international drug trafficking dwarfed the problem of Colombia's internal political strife. Today, Colombia is notorious as the major producer and exporter of cocaine—an association that has sometimes eclipsed the country's literary, theatrical, and artistic movements.

> "García Márquez has . . . confirmed his position as a rare storyteller, richly endowed with material, from imagination and experience, which seems inexhaustible."
>
> **ROYAL SWEDISH ACADEMY OF SCIENCES**

Political Unrest in the United States: Richard Nixon was president of the United States when *One Hundred Years of Solitude* was published. At the time, the United States had joined international efforts to combat underground terrorist organizations in the Middle East, faced the ramifications of military coups in Latin America, and coped with Vietnam protestors. The anti-war protests on college campuses came to a head in 1970 at Kent State, when the Ohio National

Guard was called in to restore order, and shot to death four unarmed students. Today, political protesters in the United States rally around labor movements in Mexico and Latin America. According to liberal observers, the conservative NAFTA treaty rewards only the white-owned companies that employ native workers, and not the workers themselves. Opponents of NAFTA champion goods made in Latin America by Latin American companies.

García Márquez in Context

His Influences and Impact

When *One Hundred Years of Solitude* was published in 1967, Latin American literature was in the midst of a new renaissance called "El Boom." García Márquez was always associated with the literary movement, but it was not until the publication of *One Hundred Years of Solitude* that he became a figure of central importance to El Boom.

El Boom began in 1959, shortly after the Cuban Revolution. The movement included such writers as the celebrated Argentinean poet, essayist, and short-story writer **Jorge Luis Borges** (1899–1986), author of *Ficciones* (1945), and Mexico's **Carlos Fuentes** (b. 1928), author of the immensely popular *The Death of Artemio Cruz* (1964). Another writer from Argentina, **Julio Cortázar** (1914–1984), was also at the forefront of the literary revolution. Cortázar's novels often dispense with the notion of linear time. The Guatemalan writer **Miguel Ángel Asturias**

> "Faulkner is a writer who has had much to do with my soul, but Hemingway is the one who had the most to do with my craft — not simply for his books, but for his astounding knowledge of the aspect of craftsmanship in the science of writing."
>
> **GABRIEL GARCÍA MÁRQUEZ**

The Life of Gabriel García Márquez

(1899–1974), winner of the 1967 Nobel Prize for Literature, stunned Latin America with his surrealist novel *The President* (1946). But no one equaled the magical, epic success that García Márquez attained with *One Hundred Years of Solitude*. His later novels have received critical and popular accolades, and many writers working today have been influenced by García Márquez's innovations, including Günter Grass, John Fowles, and Isabel Allende.

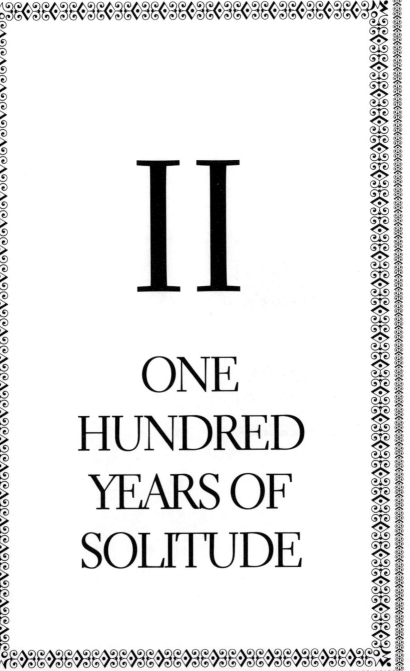

II

ONE HUNDRED YEARS OF SOLITUDE

One Hundred Years of Solitude

An Overview

🌿

Key Facts

Genre: Tragicomic epic

First Publication: *Cien Años de Soledad,* 1967 (trans. *One Hundred Years of Solitude,* 1970)

Setting: The 1820s–1930s in Macondo, a fictional village, and in an unnamed city in Colombia, South America

Narrator: Omniscient (all-knowing) third-person

Plot Overview: The novel chronicles the rise of the Buendía family in the jungles of Colombia around 1820, and its fall one hundred years later. Over the span of a century, the village founded by José Arcadio Buendía is plagued by everything from corrupt politicians to pestilential dust storms. The Buendía family continually intertwines with near-incestuous sexual couplings and births, which climax with the birth and death of a boy with a pig's corkscrew tail.

Style, Technique, and Language

Style—Magical Realism: The most prominent characteristic of Gabriel García Márquez's style is his use of fantastic and absurd elements in an otherwise believable, realistic story. This technique is called magical realism. An early example of magical elements in the novel comes when José Arcadio Buendía and his wife, Úrsula, are driven away from their home by a magical ghost who tries to plug up a hole in its throat with grass. While the ghost and its grass plug are absurd, García Márquez submits them to us in all seriousness. They are presented as a realistic part of the story, and they evoke sympathy and fear, not laughter or disbelief.

Fantastic elements recur throughout the novel, from Úrsula's fourteen-month pregnancy to the fate of the last Buendía, who is born with the tail of a pig. But the accumulation of absurd details does not overwhelm the believability of the plot. García Márquez places the magical touches sparingly among the mostly realistic stories, which include a harrowing journey to Macondo on foot and the exploitation of native goods and resources by outsiders.

Technique—Hyperbole and Allegory: García Márquez performs his feats of magical realism largely by using **hyperbole**, or dramatic exaggeration. His fanciful hyperboles include an enormous chunk of ice that José Arcadio Buendía believes to be a diamond, a magnifying glass the size of a drum, a forest of flowers, an enormous penis belonging to José Arcadio II, an amazingly gluttonous elephant woman, and a plague of insomnia. In addition to hyperbole, García Márquez uses **allegory**, a technique in which events or people stand for something outside the narrative. The fate of Macondo is an allegory for the fate of Latin American countries. Like Macondo, Latin American countries have suffered at the hands of priests, colonialists, civil wars, and exploitative outsiders.

Language—Reading in Translation: The English translation of One Hundred Years of Solitude approximates the dazzling quality of García Márquez's language. Although all translations necessarily fall short of communicating the exact voice of the original author, Gregory Rabassa, who has translated most of García Márquez's works into English, possesses a masterful command of the nuances of García Márquez's style. It was Rabassa's translation of *One Hundred Years of Solitude* that cinched his reputation as a peerless translator. Rabassa was born in 1922 in Yonkers, New York, and graduated from Columbia University. He has translated most of the outstanding novels from the El Boom renaissance in Latin American fiction, including works by García Márquez, Mario Vargas Llosa, Jorge Amadio, Julio Cortázar, and Miguel Angel Asturias.

Characters in
One Hundred Years of Solitude

Aureliano Babilonia: The illegitimate son of Mauricio Babilonia and Renata Remedios (Meme). A nun brings him to the Buendía home from the cloister where his mother died. He has a baby with his aunt, Amaranta. This baby, Aureliano Buendía, is born with a pig's tail.

Mauricio Babilonia: The father of Aureliano Babilonia, whom he has with Renata Remedios (Meme). He is mistaken for a chicken thief and shot while trying to climb in Meme's bathroom window.

Amaranta Buendía: The daughter of the Buendía patriarch, José Arcadio Buendía, and his wife, Úrsula.

Amaranta Úrsula Buendía: The daughter of Fernanda del Carpio and Aureliano Segundo Buendía. Amaranta becomes the lover of her nephew, Aureliano Babilonia, and has a baby with him. This baby, Aureliano Buendía, is born with a pig's tail as a result of his incestuous parentage.

José Arcadio Buendía: The founder of Macondo and patriarch of the Buendía family, he leaves his original home because he is being pursued by the ghost of a man he killed during a fight. Úrsula and José are cousins, a blood relationship that makes Úrsula fear she will bear a child born with a pig's tail. After Macondo is established, José Arcadio Buendía becomes obsessed with the marvels of modern scientific progress, which are brought to him by the gypsies. He dies senile and disillusioned, tied to a tree in the backyard.

Colonel Aureliano Buendía: The second son of José Arcadio Buendía and Úrsula. Tall and bookish, Aureliano becomes a fierce Liberal leader in his country's civil wars after observing local corruption. His brother, José Arcadio II Buendía, saves him from the firing squad. Aureliano spends his last years making small golden fish and dies in solitude, totally disillusioned.

Aureliano Buendía: The son born to Amaranta Úrsula Buendía and her nephew and lover, Aureliano Babilonia. Because his parents are incestuous lovers, Aureliano Buendía is born with the tail of a pig, a curse greatly feared by his great-great-great grandmother, Úrsula Buendía. After Aureliano Buendía dies, ants carry away his body, while his dead mother lies motionless, and his drunken father watches in stunned disbelief.

Gabriel García Márquez

Aureliano José Buendía: The son of Pilar Ternera and Colonel Aureliano Buendía, he falls in love with his aunt, Amaranta, and leaves home to help his father fight against the Conservatives. He is killed in battle.

Aureliano Segundo Buendía: The son of José Arcadio III Buendía and Santa Sofía de la Piedad, and the twin of José Arcadio IV Segundo Buendía. At first a bookish child, as was his great-uncle the Colonel, Aureliano Segundo eventually becomes obsessed with food and sex. He marries the frigid beauty Fernanda del Carpio, but associates mostly with his longtime mixed-race lover, Petra Cotes.

José Arcadio II Buendía: The son of the Buendía patriarch, José Arcadio Buendía, and his wife, Úrsula. José Arcadio II is born on the way to Macondo. As a teenager, José Arcadio II develops an enormous penis and fathers a child, José Arcadio III Buendía, by the mixed-race gypsy woman Pilar Ternera. Pilar also has a baby, Aureliano José, by José Arcadio II Buendía's brother, the Colonel. José Arcadio II saves the Colonel from a firing squad during the civil wars that tear his city apart. His own death is a mystery; it is unclear whether he commits suicide or is murdered.

José Arcadio III (Arcadio) Buendía: The son of José Arcadio II and Pilar Ternera, he is the first grandchild of Úrsula and the Buendía patriarch, José Arcadio Buendía. As a young man, José Arcadio III seems kind and gentle, but when he is put in charge of Macondo during a civil war, even his grandmother agrees that he becomes a vicious despot. With Santa Sofía de la Piedad, José Arcadio III sires Remedios the Beauty and twins, Aureliano Segundo and José Arcadio IV Segundo.

José Arcadio IV Segundo Buendía: The son of José Arcadio III Buendía and Santa Sofía de la Piedad, and the twin of Aureliano Segundo Buendía. Unlike his twin brother, who gorges on food and sex, José Arcadio IV becomes obsessed with civil rights and leads a workers' strike against the banana company. In the massacre that follows, he is the only survivor. He returns after seeing a train-load of corpses and discovers that no one in Macondo remembers anything about the massacre. He takes refuge in the room containing the gypsy Melquíades' old manuscripts.

José Arcadio V Buendía: The son of Aureliano Segundo Buendía and Fernanda del Carpio. An eccentric little boy, he is reared largely by the ancient Úrsula Buendía. When José Arcadio V is an adolescent, Úrsula dresses him in a green corduroy suit with copper buttons, ties a bow around his neck, and sends him off to Rome so that he can study in a seminary and become Pope. He returns to the Buendía family obsessed with inheriting its wealth, which has deteriorated to nothing but pesos. He does find Úrsula's hidden gold, but a group of children drown him during an orgy.

Renata Remedios Buendía (Meme): The daughter of Aureliano Segundo Buendía and Fernanda del Carpio, she bears an illegitimate son, Aureliano Babilonia, by Mauricio Babilonia.

Úrsula Buendía: The matriarch of the Buendía family and the wife of José Arcadio Buendía, she lives well over a hundred years. She sees the rise of Macondo and the gradual disintegration of the family. Úrsula pins her hopes on José Arcadio V, who she believes can become Pope.

Fernanda Del Carpio: Gorgeous and cold, she marries Aureliano Segundo Buendía and with him has three children: Renata Remedios (Meme), José Arcadio, and Amaranta Úrsula.

Petra Cotes: The mixed-race lover of Aureliano Segundo Buendía. Her chemistry with Aureliano Segundo is so powerful that it incites farm animals to copulate.

Melquíades: A gypsy, he brings the first modern marvels to Macondo—the magnets, the astrolabe, and the magnifying glass. A magical creature, he fascinates the Buendía patriarch, José Arcadio Buendía. Melquíades dies, but reappears to succeeding generations of Buendías. He leaves his books and manuscripts at the Buendía home, and we eventually learn that these books contain the history of the Buendía family and foretell their doom.

Don Apolinar Moscote: A magistrate of the central government, he brings soldiers to Macondo and threatens to unseat Macondo's patriarch, José Arcadio Buendía.

Remedio Moscote: The daughter of Don Apolinar Moscote. She marries Colonel Aureliano Buendía, but dies soon after the wedding due to complications during a pregnancy.

Santa Sofía De La Piedad: The wife of José Arcadio III. With him, she has Remedios the Beauty and the twins Aureliano Segundo and José Arcadio IV Segundo.

Pilar Ternerna: She has a son, Aureliano José Buendía, with Colonel Aureliano Buendía. She has another son, José Arcadio III Buendía, with José Arcadio II Buendía, who is Colonel Aureliano Buendía's brother.

Rebeca: Second cousin to Úrsula, she has green skin and eats paint chips and dirt.

The Buendía Family Tree

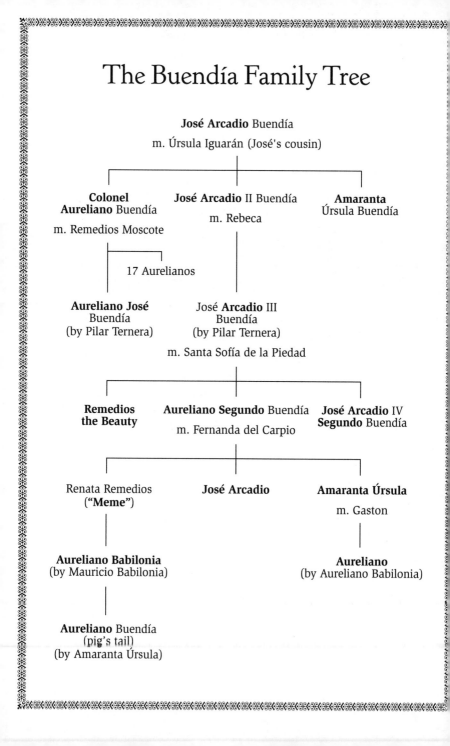

José Arcadio Buendía
m. Úrsula Iguarán (José's cousin)

Colonel Aureliano Buendía
m. Remedios Moscote

José Arcadio II Buendía
m. Rebeca

Amaranta Úrsula Buendía

17 Aurelianos

Aureliano José Buendía
(by Pilar Ternera)

José **Arcadio** III Buendía
(by Pilar Ternera)
m. Santa Sofía de la Piedad

Remedios the Beauty

Aureliano Segundo Buendía
m. Fernanda del Carpio

José Arcadio IV **Segundo** Buendía

Renata Remedios
(**"Meme"**)

José Arcadio

Amaranta Úrsula
m. Gaston

Aureliano Babilonia
(by Mauricio Babilonia)

Aureliano
(by Aureliano Babilonia)

Aureliano Buendía
(pig's tail)
(by Amaranta Úrsula)

One Hundred Years of Solitude

Reading *One Hundred Years of Solitude*

🌿

CHAPTERS 1–4
Chapter 1

The narrator explains the history of the village called Macondo. **José Arcadio Buendía**, his wife, **Úrsula**, their young son, and a few friends cleared a small area in an untouched part of the jungle. They built twenty adobe huts for their families. It was clean and quiet, and the people smelled of sweet basil and solitude. By the time a few years had passed, more than three hundred people lived in Macondo. No one was over thirty, and no one had died. During the day, choruses of canaries, redbreasts, and beautifully plumed troupials serenaded the people. Everyone enjoyed the birdsong except Úrsula. She plugged her ears with wax so that she could divide the hypnotic magic of the bird songs from the earthy realities of cooking and cleaning.

The bird songs bring the gypsies to Macondo. Every March, they set up their ragged tents. One day, José Arcadio Buendía becomes mesmerized by their scientific curiosities, objects that no one in Macondo has ever seen before. José Arcadio Buendía buys magnets, an astrolabe, a compass, a sextant, and some old maps. He shuts himself away, obsessed with alchemy and knowledge. He makes small progress, seizing an orange and declaring that the world is round, and using his magnets to unearth a fifteenth-century suit of armor from beneath a riverbed. Inside the armor, he finds a skeleton wearing a locket that contains a lock of hair. His wife, Úrsula, along with the entire village, believes he has gone mad.

"For other writers, I think, a book is born out of an idea, a concept. I always start with an image....When I was a very small boy in Aracataca, my grandfather took me to the circus to see a dromedary. Another day, when I told him I hadn't seen the ice on show, he took me to the banana company's settlement, asked them to open up a crate of frozen mullet and made me put my hand in. The whole of *One Hundred Years of Solitude* began with that one image.

GABRIEL GARCÍA MÁRQUEZ

Not content with alchemy and disappointing scientific experiments, José Arcadio Buendía studies old maps belonging to **Melquíades**, a gypsy. José Arcadio intuitively grasps the possibility that a world of knowledge, far different from Macondo, exists beyond the jungle. He recruits a team of men and begins hacking a path through the jungle, through the swamps, and over formidable mountains, determined to discover this new world of scientific enlightenment. Almost two years later, José Arcadio Buendía and his team return in frustration. However, they set out on a new adventure and stumble onto the skeleton of a Spanish galleon, marooned in the forest. They return to Macondo, fearing that perhaps there is no great city of knowledge after all.

Back in Macondo, Úrsula has been busy conferring with other wives, and when her husband returns, she announces they should stay put, begin dying, and start establishing continuity with generations of Buendías. She has children who need a father at home. Reluctantly, José Arcadio Buendía admits to the wisdom of his wife's ultimatum. His oldest son, José Arcadio Buendía II, is fourteen, and his son Aureliano will be six in March. Aureliano, who wept in Úrsula's womb, has been predicting the future since he was three years old.

The gypsies return, and José Arcadio Buendía takes his sons to see a miracle: the biggest diamond in the world. One of the gypsies mutters that the diamond is ice. Years later, Aureliano remembers this moment as he faces a firing squad.

Chapter 2

Before the founding of Macondo, Úrsula deeply feared the consequences of incest, for José Arcadio Buendía, her husband, is also her cousin. Úrsula's aunt, who had married a Buendía, gave birth to a child with a pig's tail, and Úrsula worried that someday another Buendía would be born with a pig's tail. Úrsula wanted to escape her fears and the city where her aunt had given birth to the deformed child, so she urged her husband to leave their home in Riohacha and find a new home for them. Unlike his wife, José Arcadio Buendía was unconcerned about the curse of incest. If Úrsula birthed piglets, he hoped that they could talk. This humorous boasting made Úrsula even more fearful. She began wearing a leather chastity belt fastened with an iron padlock, relinquishing it only after José Arcadio Buendía killed a man, Prudencio Aguilar, who mocked his sexual potency.

After killing Aguilar, José Arcadio Buendía thrust a spear into the dirt floor of their bedroom and demanded to have sex with his wife. Later, the ghost of Prudencio Aguilar took up residence in the Buendía household and became a pest, using grass to try to plug up the hole in his throat. This ghost was the last straw, and José Arcadio Buendía and Úrsula abandoned their home and set out to establish a new village. Heavy with a pregnancy that was to last for a fantastical fourteen months, Úrsula had to be carried in a hammock during the second half of the trip.

Úrsula gives birth to a son, **José Arcadio II**, on the journey to the new village. José Arcadio does not have a pig's tail. He does, however, sprout a prodigious penis when he is a teenager, and the narrator tells us that eventually he succumbs to the wiles of the fortune-teller **Pilar Ternera**, who becomes pregnant with his child. Later, José Arcadio II falls in love with another woman, a very young and very beautiful gypsy girl. One night, wrapping a red cloth around his head, José Arcadio II leaves with his young love and the gypsies. Úrsula becomes hysterical at the thought that her son has become a gypsy. José Arcadio Buendía apathetically comments that perhaps his son will learn to be a man.

Desolate at losing her oldest son, Úrsula abandons her newborn daughter, **Amaranta Buendía**, and sets out to coax José Arcadio II back home. She fails to

THE PIG-TAILED BABY

The Buendía child born with a pig's tail is partly a fantasy, and partly the embodiment of fears of incest. It is also, however, partly realistic. Newborns can emerge with small tails as a result of genetic atavism, which is the appearance of a peculiar physical trait typical of an earlier ancestral characteristic. Atavism can also cause babies to be born with gill slits behind their ears or with a covering of thick, dark hair. Specific behaviors are sometimes attributed to this genetic recombination; for example, some psychologists believe that serial killers are victims of atavism.

Fig. 25

Fig. 24

find her son, but five months after leaving, she returns with strangers. Amazingly, she has found a two-day route from the sea to civilization. The world and the future lies only two days away.

Chapter 3

In time, the abandoned Pilar Ternera gives birth to the son of José Arcadio II, **José Arcadio III**, whom she calls "Arcadio." Úrsula grudgingly accepts the baby into the family. Before long, a second cousin of Úrsula's joins the Buendía family. This new arrival is **Rebeca**, eleven years old and green-skinned. She carries her parents' bones in a sack and obsessively eats dirt from the courtyard and chips of whitewash from the side of the adobe house. She is cured of her eating disorder, but then catches the insomnia plague, a disease that causes people in Macondo to forget the names of objects.

José Arcadio Buendía tries to label everything to combat the quickly spreading plague of insomnia. The villagers suffering from the plague are awake, but their consciousnesses seem to be sleeping. After attempting to quarantine the town by putting bells at its entrance, José Arcadio Buendía resolves to create a "memory machine"—a primitive computerlike device that contains a dictionary of words—before he too falls into a never-ending, silent insomnia. He compiles over 14,000 entries before Melquíades, the old gypsy, returns to Macondo and offers José Arcadio Buendía a drink from one of his flasks. At this, a light goes on in Buendía's fading memory. Macondo celebrates. The plague is over.

Macondo, now in touch with civilization, receives a visit from **Don Apolinar Moscote**, a magistrate of the central government who brings soldiers and threatens to unseat José Arcadio Buendía. In the meantime, the slim and serious Buendía son Aureliano becomes captivated by Moscote's youngest daughter, **Remedios**.

Chapter 4

One night, a sexually frustrated Aureliano seeks out Pilar Ternera, sleeps with her, and impregnates her. Amaranta and Rebeca become rivals. Both love Pietro Crespi, a blond, handsome piano builder from the outside world. Rebeca returns to eating dirt after Amaranta threatens her with death. In the midst of this seething sexuality, Pilar Ternera, who bore Arcadio, the child fathered by José Arcadio II, announces that she is pregnant with a child fathered by Aureliano, the brother of José Arcadio II. The gypsy Melquíades falls ill, and a thin moss coats his skin. He dies.

José Arcadio Buendía, patriarch of the family, goes mad, wracked with sadness after the death of Melquíades and terrorized by the ghost of the murdered Prudencio Aguilar. José Arcadio slits the throats of his prized fighting cocks in order to appease the ghost. Eventually, Buendía is tied to a chestnut tree in the backyard, where he barks in Latin and drools green froth.

UNDERSTANDING AND INTERPRETING
Chapters 1–4

Macondo as Eden: Macondo shares some of the features and flaws of the biblical Eden. There are some differences between Macondo and Eden; unlike Adam and Eve, who know no sadness, José Arcadio Buendía and Úrsula are familiar with fear and unhappiness. They strike out for the jungle in order to flee a ghost and the consequences of incest. However, like Adam and Eve, the Buendías settle in a peaceful, beautiful place. In Macondo, as in Eden, death is unknown, for none of the inhabitants of Macondo have passed away. Into this idyll comes temptation in the form of knowledge, just as in Eden the snake tempts Eve with fruit from the forbidden Tree of Knowledge. Gypsies, attracted to Macondo by its symphonic birdsong, tempt José Arcadio Buendía with amazing objects, bringing magnets, astrolabes, compasses, magnifying glasses, and sewing machines. Knowledge so intoxicates José Arcadio Buendía that he begins to isolate himself in his laboratory. He sets out with a few followers to look for a civilized city so that the people of Macondo can be freed from their jungle isolation, but finds no route to the outside world. It is Úrsula who eventually stumbles upon a route to civilization. After Úrsula's discovery, 1820s modernity invades Macondo and changes its once-solitary quality of life.

Leaping Back and Forth in Time: García Márquez does not tell the story of the Buendía family in a linear, chronological manner. Instead, he jumps back and forth in time, telling us what Aureliano is thinking as he faces a firing squad, and then telling us about the origins of Aureliano's family (our synopsis of the chapters is chronological, to avoid confusion). García Márquez moves back to a few years after the founding of Macondo, introducing the gypsies, then moves even further back in time to the founding of Macondo, and then sails forward to José Arcadio Buendía's attempt to discover a city of knowledge in the world beyond the jungle. He weaves his narrative back and forth, beyond and behind, while lacing it with fantastic characters and events. Flashbacks do not briefly distract us from the main plot; rather, no one main plot exists, and each nonsequential scene matters equally. García Márquez creates a narrative that resembles a series of shuffled photographs, each photograph containing its own story.

García Márquez's Magical Realism: García Márquez writes tales of magical realism, a mode in which moments of fantasy are treated as realistic. Magical realism differs from fantasy because it does not portray a wholly fantastical world, but a largely everyday, realistic world in which magical things occasionally happen. For example, in José Arcadio Buendía's realistic quest for knowledge, his supernaturally strong magnets unearth a fifteenth-century suit of armor from beneath a riverbed. Other magical touches include the never-ending symphony of bird songs, the skeleton of a Spanish galleon filled with a forest of exotic flowers, and Aureliano, the child who weeps in his mother's womb and foretells the future at age three. The baby born long ago with a pig's tail is a frightening, supernatural symbol of punishment for incest, as is the monumental penis of the teenaged José Arcadio II. Marquez shades even tiny details with fantasy: asthmatic hens rasp and cough, gypsies produce a flying carpet, and a pan of water boils without any fire under it. Green-skinned Rebeca carries the bones of her parents in a bag, an insomnia plague wipes away the memories of Macondo's inhabitants, and as Melquíades grows weaker, moss covers his skin. Marquez presents all of these fantastical moments and people as actual occurrences, an unremarkable and natural part of life. The people of Macondo do not comment on the magic in their lives, for they do not see it as magic.

> "The world is the familiar García Márquez world, a mixture of phantasmagoria and a realism whose truths seem as incredible and strange as the moments of demonic magic."
>
> A. S. BYATT

CHAPTERS 5–9

Chapter 5

Chapters 5 through 9 center on José Arcadio Buendía's second son, Aureliano—the first baby born in Macondo. In contrast to José Arcadio II, José Arcadio Buendía's first son and the possessor of a majestic penis, Aureliano was shy and had the gift of supernatural prophecy when he was young. As an adult, he fell in love with nine-year-old Remedios Moscote and had sex with Pilar Ternera, by whom he fathered a son, Aureliano José.

BLOOD SACRIFICE

Primitive societies sometimes believe in a
Supreme Power who demands regular
blood sacrifices as payment for answering
prayers. Appropriate sacrificial victims
include treasured people or animals. Often
the blood sacrifice is a prized animal, a
virgin daughter, or a father's most beloved
son. When José Arcadio Buendía and his
wife, Úrsula, almost go mad, persecuted by
the ghost of the man Buendía stabbed
through the throat with a spear, Buendía
slits the throats of his prized fighting cocks
in order to appease the ghost and convince
it to leave the Buendía family in peace.

Gabriel García Márquez

This section of the novel begins in March, the month when the gypsies used to make their annual trip to Macondo with new technological marvels. Aureliano and Remedios, who plan to marry, are very happy. Flowers abound, rockets fire, and the music of several bands rings out in Macondo. Remedios, the bride, behaves thoughtfully after the ceremony. She takes the largest piece of wedding cake to her father-in-law, the old and senile José Arcadio Buendía, who is still tied to the chestnut tree in the backyard.

> "It is not easy to describe the techniques and themes of the book without making it sound absurdly complicated, labored and almost impossible to read. In fact, it is none of these things."
>
> **ROBERT KIELY**

The people of Macondo feel they do not need a priest, but despite this, a Catholic priest moves to Macondo and begins raising money for what he hopes will be the largest church in the world. He tries to prove the existence of God to his flock by drinking thick, hot chocolate and levitating six inches off the ground. Money begins to pile up in the church coffers. Rebeca is one of the priest's earliest converts. She hopes for a speedy marriage to Pietro Crespi, despite Amaranta's threats.

Tragedy strikes the Buendía family when little Remedios, who has adopted Aureliano José, her husband's child by Pilar Ternera, becomes pregnant with twins. The twins cross in her womb, and Remedios dies three days later.

Mourning for Remedios pauses when something shakes the Buendía house. An enormous, cryptically tattooed, bison-necked man arrives, his shoulders barely able to pass through a doorway. The huge man is José Arcadio II, who has returned. After eating sixteen raw eggs, he sleeps for three days, then grandly enters the general store. There he exhibits his enormous penis, which has intricate tattoos in several languages, and starts a raffle. He says the winner of the raffle will get to sleep with him, but in the end he sleeps with all the women. José Arcadio II becomes a legend. When he passes gas, flowers wilt.

Later, the earth-eating Rebeca passes the bedroom of José Arcadio II and realizes that compared to this mass of masculinity, the pretty Pietro Crespi has the sex appeal of a sugary gingerbread man. Not long afterward, José Arcadio II lifts her into a hammock and takes her virginity, while she silently thanks God. Three days later, they marry.

Politics and the ongoing civil war between Liberals and Conservatives infiltrate Macondo and affect Aureliano Buendía. In theory, the Liberals are Freemasons, insist on the legitimacy of civil marriages and divorces, and recognize the rights of illegitimate children. Conservatives, on the other hand, are self-defined men of God who champion family values. While playing dominoes one night with his Conservative father-in-law, Don Apolinar Moscote, Aureliano observes Moscote's corruption. He watches Moscote switch ballots in the voting box, ensuring his own election as Conservative mayor. Aureliano instantly decides to become a Liberal. Civil war breaks out, a Conservative army garrison is set up, martial law is declared, and a curfew is established. War has come to Macondo.

Chapter 6

Rallying friends, Aureliano proclaims himself a colonel and quickly leads village rebels in rousting the Conservative commander out of Macondo. He then gathers his rebel forces and heads for the countryside to join the war. In his absence, he leaves his nephew Arcadio (José Arcadio Buendía III) in command of Macondo. Arcadio becomes a bloodthirsty despot. Only his grandmother, Úrsula, dares to cross him. Eventually, Úrsula rules the town, weeping privately to the now almost autistic patriarch, José Arcadio Buendía, that violence has decimated all the promises they made to themselves and all their hopes for their children.

Meanwhile, incestuous longings continue to simmer among the Buendías. José Arcadio III lusts after his mother, Pilar Ternera, just as his father and his uncle lusted after her. Pilar senses the lust her son feels for her, and she fools him. She tells her son she will sleep with him one night, but instead of going to his room as promised, she pays her entire life savings to a virgin to go in her place. The virgin is **Santa Sofía de la Piedad**. Santa Sofía soon gives birth to a daughter, **Remedios**, and later, she produces twins, **José Arcadio Segundo** and **Aureliano Segundo**.

The Liberals lose control of the town, and José Arcadio III is shot at dawn.

Chapter 7

Out in the jungle, Colonel Aureliano is jailed. Úrsula visits him and, to her surprise, finds that he knows about all of the tragedies that have befallen the Buendía family since he left. Aureliano must face a firing squad. At the moment he anticipates a volley of bullets, he remembers his father and the wonderful "invention of ice." Suddenly, the gigantic José Arcadio II approaches the firing squad with a fearsome-looking shotgun and saves his brother. Colonel Aureliano Buendía then reinstates himself as commander of the Liberal forces. He is soon defeated more than thirty times, but he comforts himself by remembering that he fights for a just cause.

THE BLOODY WARS OF COLOMBIA

Wars have torn apart Colombia ever since the Spanish settled the country in the early 1700s and slaughtered the indigenous people who resisted domination. Colombia began rising up against Spain in 1810, and its struggle to gain independence lasted for nine years. In 1819, Simón Bolívar finally liberated Colombia from Spain. Greater Colombia eventually disintegrated when, in 1830, Venezuela and Ecuador became separate nations. Later, conflict broke out in Colombia between two opposing political factions, the Liberals and the Conservatives. Each party boasted of the superiority of its values, the Liberals siding with populist ideals and the Conservatives with the moneyed classes and traditional family values. When one civil war ended, the winning party usually installed a fiercely repressive government.

Sometime later, back in Macondo, José Arcadio II returns home with a brace of rabbits. He goes into the bedroom, and his wife, Rebeca, hears a pistol shot. A thin stream of blood trickles under the closed bedroom door, flows out the front door, and winds through the neighborhood to his mother's kitchen. Úrsula screams. Intuitively, she knows that her son is dead.

Chapter 8

Aureliano José, the child of Pilar Ternera and Colonel Aureliano Buendía, has grown to manhood. His aunt Amaranta watches him shave and marvels at his resemblance to his father. Aureliano José and Amaranta sleep in the same bed and make love during the night. Later, Aureliano José leaves to join the Liberals.

The Macondo school gets rebuilt, and Remedios and Santa Sofia's twins enroll. Despite her advanced age, Úrsula opens a pastry shop and makes a fortune in gold, which she stuffs in gourds and hides under the bedroom floor. Aureliano José returns and demands to marry his aunt. Amaranta refuses, citing the immorality of such an arrangement, and the danger that their children would be born with pigs' tails. In the meantime, seventeen illegitimate sons of Colonel Aureliano begin trickling into Macondo. All of the sons are named Aureliano, and all of them bring their own sons, who are of all colors and races.

Colonel Aureliano Buendía returns with a thousand men and wrests control of the town from the Conservative general. He orders the execution of all of the Conservative officers, despite Úrsula's plea to spare the kindhearted General José Raquél Moncada.

Chapter 9

Colonel Aureliano Buendía is disillusioned and fed up with war, but he returns to battle, this time in an attempt to halt the ravenous, warmongering Liberals. When he returns home, he has a fever, and sores cover him. Úrsula sees how thoroughly war has destroyed her remaining son. The Colonel shoots himself, but fails to hit a vital organ. He survives and retires to his workshop, where he spends the rest of his life making little gold fish.

Chapters 5–9

Machismo and Sexual Appetite: The term "machismo" connotes a state of bristling male aggression—aggression toward other men, and dominance and sexual aggression toward women. Machismo demands that insults to one's manhood be revenged. When Prudencio Aguilar says José Arcadio is less of a man than one of his fighting cocks, for example, machismo obligates José Arcadio to respond, which he does by killing Prudencio with a spear and then raping his wife, Úrsula, at spear-point. Men with machismo attach little importance to the sexual rights of women, as we see when José Arcadio II casually deserts Pilar Ternera after sleeping with her, and his brother Aureliano needlessly uses Pilar to work off his sexual frustration, since he cannot sleep with nine-year-old Remedios Moscote.

The most obvious symbol of the Buendía men's machismo is the colossal penis of José Arcadio II. At the same time, however, José Arcadio II's penis undercuts the total dominance of the macho man. Machismo makes women into sex objects, but José willingly makes himself into a sex object by selling his body. The dominance of machismo is lessened by José's willingness to turn himself into a plaything for women and by the evidence that women, like men, have voracious sexual appetites.

Disillusioned and Alone: The once-idealistic José Arcadio Buendía is disappointed by the promise of scientific progress and disillusioned when his village falls victim to the insomnia plague and people begin to forget the past. Eventually, he realizes that the outside will inevitably seep into the isolated village he founded. This realization devastates the patriarch of the Buendía family. Technology sinks deep roots into Macondo, Arab merchants and Yankees arrive, and various foreigners long to use Macondo's raw materials in order to make themselves rich at Macondo's expense. José Arcadio Buendía becomes less personally powerful, too. Don Apolinar Moscote rides into town, issuing edicts and proclamations,

> **"O***ne Hundred Years of Solitude* is the first piece of literature since the Book of Genesis that should be required reading for the entire human race. It takes up not long after Genesis left off and carries through to the air age, reporting on everything that happened in between with more lucidity, wit, wisdom, and poetry that is expected from 100 years of novelists, let alone one man."
>
> **WILLIAM KENNEDY**

and the slippery, beautiful Pietro Crespi charms the young Buendía women with his piano expertise. So disillusioned does José Arcadio become that he takes refuge in madness. He lives out his old age tied to a tree in his own backyard, barking in Latin.

In an emphasis and echo of José Arcadio's madness, José's son Colonel Aureliano Buendía repeats this pattern of disappointment and eventual withdrawal into solitude. The Colonel becomes disillusioned with the long siege of civil wars, returns to the Buendía home, and hides in his workshop. In a kind of circular madness, he makes small gold fish, melts them down, and makes new gold fish out of the melted gold, endlessly repeating the pattern.

Losing the Battle and Losing the War: For a long time apolitical, Colonel Aureliano becomes a fiercely committed Liberal after seeing the Conservative mayor commit blatant election fraud. This fraud so enrages Aureliano that he becomes virulently anti-Conservative, dubs himself Colonel, and leads a revolutionary force in a series of military battles that last for years. He wants to rid Macondo of all Conservatives. He loses every battle, but continues fighting, convinced of the righteousness of his cause. When Aureliano returns from the wars, he tries and fails to commit suicide. This final failure is a piteous confirmation that Aureliano cannot succeed in war, even in war against himself, and after it, he becomes a recluse.

CHAPTERS 10–12
Chapter 10

Chapters 10, 11, and 12 focus on Aureliano Segundo Buendía, the great-nephew of Colonial Aureliano Buendía and the twin brother of José Arcadio Segundo. As young children, Aureliano Segundo and José Arcadio look so similar that not even their mother can tell them apart. As adolescents, they begin to develop different interests. Aureliano Segundo, who has no liking for war and bloodshed, becomes fascinated by the laboratory of the old gypsy man, Melquíades. It was in this laboratory that the patriarch of the family searched for great knowledge. One day, Aureliano Segundo begins reading one of the old books, fascinated by its tales of magic. His great-grandmother Úrsula, now one hundred years old, comments that the old Macondo she knew is slowly coming to an end. Magic does not happen anymore in the village. However, one day, as Aureliano studies some manuscripts, magic returns: the gypsy Melquíades, who died years ago, reappears. From then on, Melquíades and Aureliano Segundo talk to each other almost every afternoon.

Gabriel García Márquez

Meanwhile, Father Antonio Isabel tutors José Arcadio Segundo in preparation for his first communion. At José's first confession, Father Isabel asks him if he has done bad things with women or animals. It has never occurred to José to do bad things with animals, but the priest's question prompts him to learn more about this particular perversion. After pestering the village sexton for information, José begins having sex with donkeys. He also begins cockfighting, breeding birds and making a good deal of money. He earns enough to pay for a prostitute. He occasionally sleeps with a woman named Petra Cotes. Petra begins sleeping with Aureliano Segundo, too, because she confuses him for José. Aureliano Segundo realizes that she has confused him and his twin, but does not correct her mistake immediately. Petra gives both twins a disease. After they are cured, José does not see her again, but Aureliano spends the rest of his life with her.

So strong is the sexual connection between Aureliano Segundo and Petra Cotes that it has magical results. Their passion for one another affects the sex lives of the farm animals: mares have triplets, hens lay eggs twice a day, and hogs seem to multiply overnight. Life is good for Aureliano Segundo. He throws lavish parties that last for days, and he becomes outlandishly wealthy.

Meanwhile, José Arcadio Segundo is obsessed with carving a channel from Macondo to the sea. He hammers at the stones in the smooth stream that ran through Macondo when it was a jungle village. He finally succeeds at his project, and the people of Macondo and some colorful visitors rush to the riverbank to see the arrival of a log raft pulled along by twenty men. This raft turns out to be both the first and the last vessel to dock in the town. A group of gaudy French prostitutes arrive on the raft. The town celebrates with a carnival, and Remedios the Beauty, the sister of the Segundo twins, is proclaimed queen.

A woman named **Fernanda del Carpio** arrives. She has been chosen as the most beautiful of the five thousand most beautiful women in the land, and she now comes to Macondo for the sole purpose of being named Queen of Madagascar. Shouting erupts, and rifle shots are fired into the fantastically costumed crowd. Many die, including some of the visitors to Macondo who watched the raft's arrival: nine clowns, three Japanese empresses, and two richly dressed royal Frenchmen.

Chapter 11

Aureliano Segundo falls under the spell of the beautiful Fernanda del Carpio and marries her, although he continues to have sex regularly with Petra Cotes. As a child, Fernanda del Carpio was told that she would grow up to be a queen, and now she believes that she has fulfilled this prophecy. Consequently, she has bowel movements only in a golden pot with the family crest on it. Occasionally, Aureliano Segundo has sex with his wife, and eventually Fernanda bears a son, **José Arcadio V**. Aureliano Segundo promises to hand over this son to his great-grandmother Úrsula, who has sworn to raise the boy to become Pope. Aureliano Segundo and Fernanda also have a daughter, and they name her **Renata Remedios Buendía**—"Meme" for short.

A short time later, the government announces another anniversary celebration of the treaty that ended the long series of civil wars. A jubilee party will take place, during which Colonel Aureliano Buendía will receive the Order of Merit. The Colonel declines the medal, and no one in his family attends the ceremony. Unexpectedly, seventeen of the Colonel's sons arrive at the Buendía home. All are illegitimate, conceived during the twenty years that the Colonel was a soldier, and all bear the name Aureliano. For three days, these Aurelianos thunderously celebrate by drinking champagne, smashing dishes, destroying rose bushes, killing hens, and dancing sad waltzes. The house shakes like a vigorous earthquake. The escapades try Fernanda del Carpio's patience, especially because Aureliano Segundo enthusiastically welcomes these sons of his great-uncle.

Two of the illegitimate Aureliano sons, Aureliano Triste and Aureliano Centeno, decide to stay in Macondo. They break into an old house, where, by chance, Rebeca is cowering with an antiquated pistol in her hand. Aureliano Triste explains that they want to rent the house. Later, he tells his family that he has seen Rebeca, and the family celebrates, glad the reclusive Rebeca has been found.

Aureliano Triste and Aureliano Centeno open up an ice factory and, before long, decide that Macondo needs a railroad. They particularly need a way to send their ice all over the countryside. Money is raised and soon a railroad comes to Macondo. Aureliano Triste rides the first train, waving from the engine of the yellow, flower-bedecked train.

GRINGOS INVADE MACONDO

Mr. Herbert and Mr. Jack Brown, founders of the banana plantation company, are gringos. "Gringo" means a white or non-Hispanic person, and in this context is a derogatory term. It does not simply refer to any white man, it refers to white men who flaunt their affluence and intend to exploit the country. The Herberts and Browns who descend on Latin America at this time use its resources to make themselves richer, pillage all they can, and depart, leaving behind the ruins.

Chapter 12

The railroad proves only the first of many marvelous, modern inventions to delight Macondo. Soon, lightbulbs and films arrive and dazzle the townspeople. Phonographs and telephones also appear. All sorts of new, oddly dressed people begin arriving. Among the strangers are two entrepreneurs, Mr. Herbert and Mr. Jack Brown. Macondo no longer resembles the original Macondo. Wooden houses shoot up, covered with zinc roofs. Gringos from North America bring their languid wives and build a separate town across the railroad tracks. Peacocks stroll on their lawns. Men change the course of the river and bring in a trainload of prostitutes. A year after Mr. Herbert's arrival, more gringos come to plant banana trees, laying the groundwork for a banana plantation.

Colonel Aureliano Buendía is tormented, for he believes the war should have been carried to its final conclusion. It particularly incenses him when a gringo casually slaughters a child and the child's grandfather. Aureliano Buendía vows to arm his sons and get rid of the gringos. Tragically, sixteen of his sons are hunted down like rabbits and shot. As Aureliano Centeno lies in a hammock one day, someone murders him, plunging an ice pick between his eyebrows. The Colonel abandons his quest and then abandons the making of his little golden fish. He returns to Melquíades' books, sinking into a miserable defeat.

UNDERSTANDING AND INTERPRETING
Chapters 10–12

Úrsula's Fantastical Hope: Úrsula's plans for José Arcadio V provide a moment of levity in the midst of the Buendías' troubles. Úrsula, now very old, has lost a husband, suffered the death of her ultra-macho first son, and seen her son the Colonel withdraw into solitude. Now, she fastens all of her hopes on the newborn José Arcadio V, son of Aureliano Segundo and Fernanda del Carpio. Taking on the task of rearing the boy, Úrsula declares that he will one day go abroad to study in a seminary in Rome, where, in due time, he will become Pope. Úrsula has absolutely no doubt that the life of José Arcadio V will progress according to her outline. It is a foregone conclusion, in her opinion: he *will* be Pope. Úrsula's plans for Arcadio V are humorous, but they also exhibit the same kind of madness and obsession that characterize most of the Buendía males.

Comedic Incest: Incestuous relationships continue to seethe in the Buendía family. Just as José Arcadio II and Aureliano shared Pilar Ternera, José Arcadio IV Segundo and his twin brother, Aureliano Segundo, share the panther-faced Petra

Cotes. Aureliano José becomes obsessed with his aunt, Amaranta, and Arcadio III becomes determined to have sex with his mother. We are not meant to react with horror to these wild couplings, however. García Márquez describes them with robust, exaggerated humor. They are cartoon versions of normal sexuality, rather than somber commentaries on realistic human behavior.

Aureliano Segundo's Strange Marriage: Aureliano Segundo is fecund in many senses of the word. He comes from the fertile Buendía family, he amasses a huge fortune, and he has an almost magical sexual relationship with Petra Cotes. Aureliano's vitality even seems to rub off on his farm animals, who reproduce at astounding rates. It seems logical that such a man would marry and begin producing a generation of new Buendías, but Aureliano defies our expectations by falling in love with the haughty carnival queen, Fernanda del Carpio, a sexually frigid woman. Fernanda does eventually give birth to three of Aureliano Segundo's children, but Aureliano never shares with her the kind of exalted sexual passion he shares with Petras Cotes, and he quickly returns to the arms of Petras.

> "Let us hope that *One Hundred Years of Solitude* will not generate one hundred years of overwritten, overlong, overrated novels."
>
> **JONATHAN BATE**

Fernanda and the Train: Fernanda and the train arrive at the same time in Macondo, and they have an identical effect on the town: they quash the unrestrained exuberance of the Buendías. Cold Fernanda dislikes sex—an attitude that clashes with the highly sexed nature of the Buendía family. The train is supposed to mean progress, but in fact it only harms Macondo, bringing passengers who will exploit the village. Its innovations clash with the original sleepy, isolated character of Macondo.

CHAPTERS 13–14
Chapter 13

Úrsula is going blind, but she continues to educate José Arcadio V so that he can journey to Rome and someday become Pope. Few people know of Úrsula's near-blindness, because she compensates for her diminished vision with her keen sense of hearing and her ability to remember the placement of furniture.

Úrsula suffers from painful ruminations. She thinks about her husband, insane and tied to a chestnut tree in the backyard, and of her first son, José Arcadio II, mad for a gypsy girl, tattooed like a tapestry and dying of a mysterious gunshot wound. She also thinks of her son the Colonel, back from the civil wars and now hiding in the solitude of his workshop.

One Thursday afternoon, José Arcadio V leaves for Rome to study at a seminary. He dresses in a green corduroy suit and wears a starched bow around his neck. Úrsula and other members of the Buendía family gather to bid him farewell. Old Colonel Aureliano sneers at the festivities, convinced that his family is mad.

Úrsula's aging daughter, Amaranta, begins sewing her own burial shroud. The gringo banana company hires José Arcadio Segundo as foreman. Fernanda continues to impose regulations on the family. The rampant materialism that has taken possession of Macondo disgusts her. Her husband, Aureliano Segundo, again begins spending nights with Petras Cotes, rarely returning home. Fernanda complains that she has become a widow, and she sends her husband two trunks of clothes. Aureliano celebrates his freedom for three days and soon grows fat. His animals multiply magically again, and stories about his gluttony eventually attract a woman who calls herself "The Elephant" and considers herself queen of all gluttons. The Elephant and Aureliano do battle, matching appetites to see who can eat the most. They wolf down slabs of beef, cartons of melons and yams, dozens of oranges and raw eggs, and a couple of hogs and roast turkeys. Aureliano Segundo loses consciousness and thus loses the contest.

Fernanda's daughter, Meme, arrives to spend a week of school vacation at home, bringing with her four nuns and sixty-eight classmates. Fernanda wails that her child is as much of a glutton for friends as Aureliano is for food. Beds must be borrowed, and seventy-two chamber pots must be purchased. In the midst of this chaos, José Arcadio IV Segundo, Úrsula's great-grandson, saunters in. He has become a drifter, sleeping here and there. Úrsula urges him to talk to the old Colonel and pry him out of his solitude. Efforts to stimulate the Colonel fail, however, until one day he rouses himself to watch a circus parade. Then he huddles against the chestnut tree in the backyard, pulls his head between his shoulders like a baby chick, and dies. The family does not find him until the following day, just as vultures are moving in on him.

Chapter 14

Meme finishes her schooling, returns home, and educates herself, learning to smoke, drink, and gossip about men. To her, Fernanda and Amaranta seem like two old ghosts from the last century. Meme becomes friends with Patricia

BANANA REPUBLICS

The fictional banana company of this novel is based on an actual business called the United Fruit Company, which brought back its first bananas from Jamaica in 1870 and sold them in Jersey City for $2 each, making a stratospheric profit. Subsequently, the United Fruit Company set up banana plantations in Guatemala, Honduras, and Colombia. These nations have often been derogatorily referred to as "banana republics" because they depend on banana exports for income. Critics have accused the United Fruit Company of influencing government officials, exploiting workers, and economically colonizing the countries it invaded.

MASSACRE IN 1928

The fictional massacre of the banana plantation workers in *One Hundred Years of Solitude* is based on an actual massacre of workers that took place in January of 1928. Striking workers were gathered in the main plaza of the city of Ciénaga when the army, sent by the Conservative party, arrived and fired on them. Hundreds of workers were killed. The Conservative party was defeated in the next election.

Brown, whose father owns the banana plantation, and she learns to swim, play tennis, gorge on Virginia ham, and speak English.

Amaranta finally finishes her shroud, and it is the most beautiful piece of needlework ever seen. She offers to take letters from the living to the dead and accumulates enough letters to fill a box, along with some verbal messages that she records in a notebook. She dies. Fernanda gives birth to a girl named **Amaranta Úrsula**.

Meme becomes the lover of **Mauricio Babilonia**, a handsome man who attracts clouds of yellow butterflies wherever he goes. Mauricio bewitches Meme, and they begin making love twice a week beneath a heavy, suffocating blanket of yellow butterflies. Their lovemaking ends abruptly when the house guard sees Mauricio Babilonia climbing into Meme's bathroom window, mistakes him for a chicken thief, and shoots him. The bullet lodges in Mauricio Babilonia's spine and paralyzes him. Eventually, Mauricio dies of solitude.

UNDERSTANDING AND INTERPRETING
Chapters 13 and 14

Empty Pockets and Loneliness: As the people of Macondo become financially impoverished, Úrsula becomes emotionally impoverished. The banana company exploits the people of Macondo and the jungle, and the company's foreign owners get rich. The old spirit that used to animate Macondo fades. Úrsula, the old matriarch of the family, fades with the town. She thinks about the human losses in her life—a husband, victim of hopelessness and madness; one son dead of unknown causes; another son isolated and obsessed with making little gold fish. Blindness worsens Úrsula's loneliness. Electricity has lighted Macondo with sudden brilliance, but Úrsula can see only a faint glow. With her loss of sight comes a loss of self. Úrsula enters an "impenetrable solitude of decrepitude."

The Colonel's Quiet Death: The Colonel's manner of death contradicts our initial assumptions. García Márquez first introduced the Colonel at the moment in his life when he stood before a firing squad. It seemed logical to assume that the Colonel would die a dramatic death by shooting. It turns out, however, that the Colonel's brother saved him from that violent end. Instead of dying dramatically, the Colonel dies as he lived: in a quiet, sad manner. The Colonel begins his life by weeping in Úrsula's womb; he fathers many children, but never loves a woman; he leads forces of Liberals against warring Conservatives, but never wins a battle. He spends his last years in solitude and dies alone, huddled against the tree where his father was tied for years.

Amaranta's Bitter Solitude: Amaranta, Úrsula's only daughter, retreats into solitude, as many Buendías have before her. In many ways, she has had a sad and difficult life. Her brother the Colonel dies alone, like a baby chick. Her brother José Arcadio II dies violently and mysteriously. The man she loves, Pietro Crespi, chooses Amaranta's half-sister, Rebeca, and later commits suicide. Her own nephew once lusted after her. As she becomes an old woman, Amaranta slowly retreats into the shadows of her memories and begins to weave her own funeral shroud. After leading such a difficult life, it is not surprising that Amaranta becomes bitter and isolated.

Moments of Levity: In these chapters, as in the rest of the novel, García Márquez mixes heartbreaking scenes with farce and scatological humor. Here, the distressing death of the Colonel is followed by an invasion of sixty-eight teenagers and four nuns. Like all of the other outsiders who have descended on the Buendías and upon Macondo, these latest invaders destroy old routines and peace of mind. After boarding school ends for the summer, Meme creates even more disruption in the Buendía household when she comes home and becomes the quintessential teenager. She smokes cigarettes and spends all of her time with the Yankee daughter of one of the men in charge of the banana company. García Márquez also makes a comic figure of the good-looking Mauricio Babilonia, who has such allure that whenever he comes to court Meme at the Buendía home, a fluttering cloud of yellow butterflies accompanies him.

Chapter 15

The shooting of Mauricio Babilonia traumatizes Meme. She ceases to wash or comb her hair and becomes mute. Fernanda takes her on a long journey to Fernanda's hometown and leaves her in a convent. A few months later, Meme gives birth to a son whom she names **Aureliano Babilonia**. An aged nun brings Aureliano to Fernanda, who is shocked at the infant's oversized penis. Fernanda locks up the boy in the old workshop where Colonel Aureliano Buendía made his small golden fish. She tells people that she found the baby in the swamp.

Armed soldiers are stationed throughout Macondo. Fernanda hears that José Arcadio IV Segundo incited workers at the banana company to strike for the right to get the day off on Sundays. The workers also want money instead of food coupons, and latrines year-round, not just at Christmastime. A strike breaks out. Telegraph and telephone wires are cut, and blood flows in irrigation ditches. The management asks workers to assemble for arbitration talks in the town square by the railroad station. More than three thousand people—workers, women, and children—gather in an open space in front of the station, waiting for government officials, who never arrive.

José Arcadio IV Segundo stands in the crowd, and he lifts up a little four-year-old boy so that the child can see. Many years later, the child will describe the horrendous massacre that took place. Machine guns suddenly fire through the crowd, slicing through bodies. Blood bathes the collapsing crowd. Many thousands die.

Afterward, the bodies are loaded on a train and taken away. José Arcadio IV Buendía has fallen unconscious, and someone tosses

"The Colonel was already an old man, making his little gold fishes, then one afternoon I thought, "Now he's had it." I had to kill him off. When I finished the chapter, I went up to [my wife] Mercedes …trembling. She knew what had happened the moment she saw my face…I lay down on my bed and cried for two hours."

GABRIEL GARCÍA MÁRQUEZ

him onto the train among the corpses. Regaining consciousness, he jumps off the train and returns to Macondo, where he finds that no one remembers anything about the massacre. According to a woman who offers him coffee, there has been no killing in Macondo since the civil wars.

Rain begins falling, ending a three-month drought, and continues falling for a week. The government maintains that no strike or massacre ever took place. Armed soldiers knock on doors, finding and killing known troublemakers. José Arcadio IV Segundo takes refuge in the old room of the gypsy Melquíades and spends the rest of his life there, reading through the old manuscripts and listening to the rain, which pours down for almost five years. The Buendía family forgets about him.

UNDERSTANDING AND INTERPRETING
Chapter 15

A Classic Buendía Baby: A number of signs suggest that Meme's son, Aureliano, will grow up in typical Buendía fashion. When the proud Fernanda hides Aureliano in the old Colonel's workshop, she exposes him to Melquíades' old manuscripts, the same manuscripts that have provided information and solace to José Arcadio Buendía, Colonel Aureliano Buendía, and, in this chapter, the dazed José Arcadio IV Segundo Buendía. Magical storytelling gets attached to

Aureliano, as it does to most of the Buendías; Fernanda tells people that she found Aureliano in a swamp, a story that echoes the biblical story of the pharaoh's daughter, who found Moses in a basket in the Nile River. Finally, Aureliano possesses a large penis, in the tradition of José Arcadio II. This physical sign of his Buendía heritage angers the prudish Fernanda and portends sexual excesses for the baby Aureliano.

A Second Plague of Forgetfulness: After the massacre of banana workers, a second bout of memory loss sweeps the town. This loss is the sequel to the first plague of forgetfulness in Macondo, which ended with the help of the gypsy Melquíades. Only José Arcadio IV Segundo escapes this second plague. Only he can remember the massacre. Immediately after thousands of citizens are gunned down, the survivors erase the incident from their memories. The whole town denies the existence of the incident. They make themselves forget in order to survive. García Márquez suggests that after a bloody disaster, some survivors cope by refusing to acknowledge what happened, preferring denial to understanding.

A Fresh Start: The rain that finally floods Macondo symbolizes a new beginning for the village. For three months, no rain has fallen on Macondo—a drought that reflects the barrenness and sterility the village feels after bartering the lives of its citizens for money from the owners of the banana company. However, after the massacre occurs and a river of blood flows from the more than three thousand dead, rain finally falls to wash away the signs of the slaughter. This flood of water exceeds even the biblical Great Flood, falling not for forty days and forty nights, but for almost five years. The deluge ushers in a symbolic fresh start for Macondo and for the survivors of the Buendía family.

CHAPTERS 16–20
Chapter 16

Rain falls for nearly five years, flooding the city. Roofs wash away, walls collapse, and every single banana tree gets uprooted. Aureliano Segundo leaves Petra Cotes, his lover of many years, and goes home to Fernanda, his wife. He begins repairing hinges, locks, doorknobs, and clocks. The great humidity in the Buendía house causes fish to swim in the windows and through the rooms.

Úrsula grows ill. Santa Sofía de la Piedad examines her and discovers that Úrsula's back is paved with black leeches. Santa Sofía removes them one by one, and Úrsula moans that as soon as the rain stops, she will die. The rain kills all of Aureliano Segundo's and Petra Cotes's magnificent breeding animals. Aureliano Segundo says nothing can be done. He plays with his daughter, Amaranta Úrsula, and little Aureliano, the son of Meme and Mauricio Babilonia, telling them stories about Colonel Aureliano Buendía, whose picture is in the encyclopedia. Occasionally, Aureliano Segundo hires diggers to search the backyard for Úrsula's fabled cache of gold.

Chapter 17

When the rains finally cease, Macondo lies in ruins. Soggy furniture and animal skeletons litter the streets. The remnants of the banana plantation are abandoned. Macondo, once an enchanted forest, is now a bog of rotting roots. Burning dust storms follow the many years of rain. Úrsula rises from her sickbed and discovers that the children have painted her face and hung dried lizards, frogs, and even rosaries on her. Termites crunch beneath the house, and leaping cockroaches plague the surviving Buendías.

Úrsula asks for the keys to the room used by the old gypsy Melquíades. She opens the door and almost dies from the stench of the seventy-two chamber pots left by Meme's guests during her school days. In the gloom, Úrsula discovers José Arcadio Segundo, the only survivor of the banana worker massacre, still reading through old manuscripts. He looks up and mutters, "Time passes."

Aureliano Segundo loses weight and moves back in with Petra Cotes. Together they open a primitive lottery business. Fernanda del Carpio enrolls Amaranta Úrsula in a private school, but keeps Aureliano, the little foundling, at home. He is delicate and thin, full of curiosity, and possessed of a clairvoyant look. He spends most of his time locked in Meme's old room. Ancient Úrsula, meantime, begins shrinking, becoming so small that she resembles a fetus. At last she is no bigger than a raisin, and has a long monkeylike paw. "My God," she gasps, "so this is what it's like to be dead." She dies on Good Friday.

The gypsies return, dragging magnets with them, and the Buendía house falls daily into deeper neglect. Meme does well in her schoolwork, and Aureliano Segundo promises to send her to Brussels to finish her studies. José Arcadio Segundo teaches little Aureliano how to read and write and begins telling him about the secrets in Melquíades' parchment papers.

Amaranta Úrsula leaves for Brussels. When the family receives her first letter, Aureliano Segundo dies. At the same moment, José Arcadio Segundo falls back from the parchments that he has been studying and dies. To ensure that they are not burying José Arcadio Segundo alive, Santa Sofía de la Piedad slits his throat with a kitchen knife. Drunken men carry out the two coffins at the same time, mix them up, and bury the brothers in the wrong graves.

Chapter 18

Aureliano, Meme's illegitimate son, remains fascinated by the old manuscripts and soon learns all of the fantastic legends by heart. As a teenager, he has as much basic knowledge as a learned medieval man. Unbeknownst to anyone, he has been talking to Melquíades and studying Sanskrit. Fernanda del Carpio believes that the house is filling up with elves and begins dressing in her moth-eaten queen's dress. She dies, covered with an ermine cape.

José Arcadio V arrives home, kisses his mother's corpse on the forehead, and, after the funeral, burns the saints that have sat on the family altar for years. He begins indulging in long, perfumed baths while dreaming of Amaranta Úrsula. He never attended the seminary in Rome. He has been living abroad in a garret and making plans to return to the grand Buendía mansion, which he has always believed would someday be his. When he returns, however, he finds squalor and ruin, and he is reduced to selling the silver candlesticks and Fernanda's golden chamber pot in order to get money for food.

José Arcadio V discovers Úrsula's gold, which consists of 7,214 pieces of eight. He lavishes some of the money on an orgy with local children, filling the

> "There are at least a half-dozen Latin American writers more deserving of the Nobel Prize: Juan Carlos Onetti, for example, or Adolfo Bioy-Casares, or [Jorge Luis] Borges. I suppose it depends on your concept of literature. If you consider the novel depends on fantasies, fine; but the philosophical depth of those older writers is absent, I'm sorry to say, in García Márquez."
>
> **ROBERTO RUIZ**

Buendía pool with champagne. One day, the mischievous children pounce on him as he lolls naked, dreaming of Amaranta. They drown him and escape with three bags of gold.

Chapter 19

Amaranta Úrsula, now a young woman, returns to Macondo with her husband Gaston, but Gaston quickly leaves. Aureliano, who has spent most of his time studying Melquíades' manuscripts, falls in love with Amaranta Úrsula. He stumbles upon his great-great-grandmother, the very old and ill Pilar Ternera, who is now manager of a combination brothel-zoo. She tells him about the grandeur and the misfortunes of the Buendía family.

Chapter 20

When Aureliano makes love to Amaranta Úrsula, he hears her laughing. They realize that they are accomplices in the tragic end of a legendary family. Over the next several months, they spend a great deal of in bed or walking around naked. At times, Amaranta Úrsula decorates Aureliano's stupendous penis, setting a little tinfoil cap on it, painting it with clown eyes, and tying an organdy bow around its shaft.

One Sunday afternoon, Amaranta Úrsula gives birth to a baby boy and discovers that he has the tail of a pig. She begins bleeding in torrents. Spiderwebs and ash are stuffed into her, but they do not help. She dies with a smile on her face. Aureliano drinks incessantly, and when he sobers up, he sees ants dragging away his infant son, who is now dead. The Buendía house begins to moan as fierce winds pull it apart. Reading Melquíades' papers, Aureliano realizes that the old gypsy foretold the rise and the fall of the Buendía family, even predicting the destruction of the house. As Aureliano reads, the roof slides off the house, and the foundation is uprooted. He reads this sentence: "*The first of the line is tied to a tree and the last is being eaten by the ants.*"

UNDERSTANDING AND INTERPRETING
Chapters 16–20

The Metamorphoses of Úrsula and Fernanda: With Macondo in ruins, two key characters undergo dramatic changes. Úrsula, for many years the commanding figure at the helm of the Buendías, finally slips into near senility, becoming little more than a plaything for the children, who drape her wasting body with dead lizards and rosaries. As she nears death, her strength and fortitude literally disappear as she shrinks down to the size of a raisin. Her metamorphosis is graphically physical. Fernanda changes greatly, too, but her change is mental. The once-haughty, emotionally anemic former carnival queen begins to fit in to the magical world around her. She even attempts to work voodoo magic on her straying husband, Aureliano Segundo, and insists that elves infest the house.

Inevitable Sexual Perversion: Úrsula's belief that José Arcadio V will become Pope proves resoundingly silly when José Arcadio V, in traditional Buendía fashion, becomes enslaved to his perverse sexual desires. He returns home a wastrel, expecting to inherit a fortune. He dies a victim of his lust for children. Just as Úrsula believed she could turn José Arcadio into a Pope, Aureliano Segundo believes that he can turn his daughter, Amaranta Úrsula, into a scholar by sending her to school in Brussels. Amaranta returns from this schooling only to fall madly, excessively, and incestuously in love—also in traditional Buendía fashion—with Aureliano, her nephew and the son of Meme and Mauricio Babilonia. Their lovemaking sessions conjure up a list of similar instances of Buendía incest or incestuous longings: José Arcadio II and Pilar Ternera, Arcadio III and his mother, Pilar Ternera, and Aureliano José and Amaranta. When Aureliano José fell hopelessly in love with his aunt Amaranta, she refused to submit to his demands, but Amaranta Úrsula does submit to the demands of Aureliano. Because the nephew and aunt have sex, the long-dreaded Buendía curse finally occurs: a baby boy is born with a pig's tail.

Conclusions

One Hundred Years of Solitude is an extremely ambitious novel. Some critics argue that its project is to sketch all of Colombian history and, more broadly, Latin America's struggles with colonialism and emergence into modernity. Although the novel is probably not meant as a straight allegory, in which every element stands for something outside the text, its histories of civil war, plantations, and labor unrest in a small town do have direct parallels in Latin American history. The novel is a rumination on specific social and historical circumstances, a tale of fiction and fantasy, and a meditation on the possibility of love and the sadness of solitude.

One Hundred Years of Solitude

One Hundred Years of Solitude was published in English in the United States three years after its initial publication in Spanish. It was almost universally acclaimed, and although it never topped the bestseller lists, it soon became a literary classic.

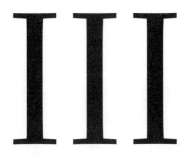

III

CHRONICLE
OF A DEATH
FORETOLD

Chronicle of a Death Foretold

An Overview

Key Facts

Genre: Psychological murder mystery

First Publication: *Crónica de una Muerte Anunciada*, 1981 (trans. *Chronicle of a Death Foretold*, 1982)

Setting: A small, unnamed coastal village in Colombia, South America; one Monday in February, around 1930, and twenty-seven years after that Monday.

Narrator: A childhood friend of the murdered man. In the last chapter, we learn that the narrator is García Márquez himself.

Plot Overview: On his wedding night, a bridegroom returns his new bride to her parents, and the family assumes that he does not want her because she is not a virgin. The bride's two drunken brothers brutally murder the man who supposedly robbed their sister of her virginity and thereby robbed the family of its honor. Twenty-seven years later, a childhood friend of the murdered man returns to the village to reconstruct the events surrounding the murder.

Style, Technique, and Language

Style—Journalistic Tone: Six years passed between the publication in 1975 of García Márquez's *Autumn of the Patriarch* and the publication of his *Chronicle of* *a Death Foretold*, in 1981. During those six years, García Márquez was busy with journalism and politics, two of his lifelong passions. Overlap between novelists, journalists, and politicians is more common in Latin America than it is in the United States; many of Latin America's most honored writers are also politicians. García Márquez, for example, was lauded as a fierce leftist politician and a remarkable journalist for *El Heraldo* and *El Espectador* long before he began writing novels. *Chronicle of a Death Foretold* utilizes the stylistic techniques of journalism. It has neither the length of other García Márquez novels, nor their lavish wealth of magic realism. Instead, the story is told in a framework of journalistic reporting, and it gains quiet, explosive power from its pared-down prose.

> "I'm fascinated by the relationship between literature and journalism. I began my career as a journalist and when I'm not working on fiction, I'm running around the world, practicing my craft as a reporter."
>
> **GABRIEL GARCÍA MÁRQUEZ**

Technique—Telling and Retelling: García Márquez bases the events of *Chronicle of a Death Foretold* on a real-life murder he read about in the newspaper. (After the publication of the novel, journalists flocked to the town of Sucre, where the events fictionalized in the novel took place.) García Márquez makes the narrator of the novel a childhood friend of the murder victim. The narrator acts almost like a journalist, investigating a murder that took place twenty-seven years prior. His narrative technique involves telling and retelling the story in an attempt to ferret out the most truthful version, first sketching out the main events, then focusing on the accuser and her bridegroom, then taking the townspeople's perspective, and finally detailing the autopsy.

Language—A Report and a Tragedy: García Márquez uses the language of journalism in part to prove that memory and language, even the purportedly objective language of a reporter, cannot provide a reliable record. Although the narrator strives to report the truth, we never quite believe that we are reading strictly objective journalism. García Márquez consciously lets slip, through the cracks of a reporter's language, a subjective story of tragedy,

Characters in
Chronicle of a Death Foretold

Father Carmen Amador: A self-centered and passive priest. When he hears that Santiago Nasar's life is in danger, he does not react, because he is too preoccupied with remembering how the bishop snubbed him. Amador decides that if Santiago is destined to be murdered, Amador can only focus on saving Santiago's departed soul.

Colonel Don Lázaro Aponte: The chubby mayor of the town. After he hears of the Vicario twins' plot to murder Santiago Nasar, he eats his breakfast of liver and onions before going to confiscate the knives that the Vicarios plan to use. He scoffs at the twins' threats, calling them "big bluffers." After viewing Santiago's butchered corpse, and later, after seeing the bungled autopsy performed by Father Amador, he becomes a vegetarian.

Clotilde Armenta: Co-owner, with her husband, of the milk shop. She is one of the narrator's best witnesses to the events surrounding the murder, for she was working in the milk shop on the morning of the crime. The twins boast about their plans in her shop on the morning of the murder, and Clotilde actively tries to prevent them from harming Santiago. She sends an urgent message for help to Father Amador, and she asks a beggar woman to warn Santiago's mother. Finally, she sells rotgut liquor to the twins, hoping that they will become too drunk to carry out their threat.

Cristo Bedoya: One of Santiago's best friends and a close friend of the narrator. He spends the night before Santiago's murder at the local whorehouse with Santiago, the narrator, and the Vicario brothers. After overhearing a remark about the murder plot, Cristo tries and fails to find Santiago. After the murder, he leaves the village and eventually becomes a renowned surgeon.

Mária Alejandrina Cervantes: The proprietress of the local whorehouse. A few years before Santiago was murdered, he worshipped Mária Alejandrina. The narrator confesses that on the morning of the murder, he himself was resting in Mária Alejandrina's lap.

Gabriel García Márquez

Divina Flor Guzmán: The daughter of the Nasars' cook, Victoria. Divina is attracted to the handsome, Arab-eyed young master of the house, but Divina's mother objects to Santiago's traditional right to have sex with her daughter. Divina is scrubbing the floor shortly before Santiago is murdered, and she has a mysterious vision of Santiago entering the house with a bouquet of roses and going up to his bedroom.

Victoria Guzmán: The Nasars' cook for many years and, at one time, the mistress of Santiago's father, old Ibrahim Nasar. Victoria slept with Ibrahim not by choice, but because as a servant, she was compelled to submit to her master's impulses. She knows about the Vicario brothers' threat to kill Santiago, but pays no heed to it. She does not care about Santiago's fate, because he threatens her daughter's virginity. The way Victoria butchers rabbits foreshadows the way the Vicario twins butcher Santiago.

Flora Miguel: Santiago's fiancée. She hears the rumor that Santiago took Angela Vicario's virginity and reacts to the news with a melodramatic outburst. When Santiago stops by her family home, she angrily returns all of the letters that he wrote to her from school and tells Santiago she hopes they kill him.

The Narrator: An old friend of Santiago. Twenty-seven years after the murder of Santiago, he returns to the small, forgotten village on the coast of Colombia to talk with villagers who remember the incident and tries to piece together the truth from their memories, legal records, old letters, and confessions. He wants to find out who was responsible for the murder and why it happened.

The Narrator's Family: The narrator's family consists of his mother, Luisa Santiaga; his father; his sister, Margot; his brother, Luis Enrique; his youngest brother, Jaime; his wife, Mercedes; and his aunt, Wenefrida.

Ibrahim Nasar: Santiago's father. He died three years before Santiago's murder. Ibrahim, an Arab, arrived in the village not long after Colombia's civil wars had drained it of money, blood, and zest for revolution. He immediately bought a warehouse near the river, planning to open an export-import business, but he ended up turning the warehouse into the family home. Ibrahim seduced Victoria Guzmán, a servant woman who worked in the stables and later became the cook for Santiago and his mother.

Plácida Linero Nasar: Santiago's mother. Despite a well-earned reputation for interpreting dreams, she fails to correctly interpret two dreams that foreshadow her son's death. Because of Divina Flor's vision of Santiago, Plácida Linero thinks that her son is already safely upstairs and so bars the front door, thereby inadvertently preventing Santiago from escaping the Vicario twins.

Santiago Nasar: The twenty-one-year-old murder victim. The Vicario twins murder Santiago because the traditional codes of virginity and machismo mandate that the man who takes an unmarried woman's virginity must be punished. Angela names Santiago as the culprit, and her word is sufficient evidence for her brothers even though there is no proof that Santiago actually deflowered her.

Alberta Simonds San Román: The mother of Bayardo San Román. After Bayardo impulsively decides to marry Angela Vicario, he brings his mother and the rest of his family to the small village so that the townspeople can see his illustrious lineage. Alberta is a mixed-race woman who, in her youth, was named the most beautiful of the two hundred most beautiful women in the Antilles. She is married to Bayardo's father, a military hero.

Bayardo San Román: Angela Vicario's bridegroom. When the thirty-one-year-old Bayardo arrives in the village, dressed in silver-spangled, skintight clothes, people wonder if he is homosexual. The rumors fade after Bayardo chooses a bride. On the night of his wedding, Bayardo returns Angela to her parents.

General Petronio San Román: Bayardo's father. When he arrives in the small coastal town ensconced in an expensive Model T Ford, the Conservative general is immediately recognized as one of the military heroes of the drawn-out civil wars of the last century. Only the narrator's mother refuses to kowtow to the general, for he gave orders for one of her ancestors, a Liberal, to be shot in the back.

Faustino Santos: The local butcher at the village meat market. He watches the Vicario twins sharpen the blades of their pig-butchering knives. Santos does not pay much attention to the twins' drunken bragging, and later says he thought they were kidding around.

Angela Vicario: Bayardo's wife. García Márquez never makes it clear why Angela maintains that Santiago Nasar took her virginity. It is possible that her accusations are false, for as a girl Angela always went about with her sisters or her mother and was virtually a prisoner in her home. On the other hand, she told her best friends that she was not a virgin. Her friends told her how to make the bridal sheets look bloody, as a virgin's would be, but she chooses not to perform this trickery. Many years later, with new prescription glasses, she again sees Bayardo, by then old and fat, and falls madly in love with him.

Gabriel García Márquez

Pablo Vicario: One of the twins who murders Santiago. He is twenty-four years old and hard-looking, but most people think him "a good sort." Pablo and his twin, Pedro, repeat their plan to murder Santiago so frequently, to so many people, that some believe the twins want someone to stop them. Pablo is the more bloody-minded of the twins. After the mayor confiscates their knives, Pedro feels that they are no longer bound to kill Santiago, but Pablo thrusts a fresh knife in Pedro's hand and drags him back to wait for Santiago. After his trial, Pablo becomes a superb goldsmith.

Pedro Vicario: One of the twins who murders Santiago. Six minutes younger than his twin brother, Pedro serves in the military while his twin stays home and takes care of the family. Pedro returns from his military stint with a painful urinary tract disease that causes him excruciating suffering on the day of Santiago's murder. After the trial, Pedro re-enlists in the military. Rumors have it that guerillas kill him.

Poncio Vicario: Angela's father. During his youth and most of his adulthood, Poncio was an acclaimed goldsmith who specialized in exquisite detail work. His extraordinary craft brought honor to his family, and he brought up his sons "to be men." He worked so long and so diligently that he became blind, and his sons had to support the family by butchering pigs. Old Poncio cuts a sad figure during his daughter's wedding celebration, sitting amidst the boisterous merrymaking while drunken guests stumble over him.

Pura Vicario: The mother of the Vicario boys. Pura worked as a schoolteacher until she married, at which time she devoted herself to her family. Along with her twin boys, she has two older daughters, a daughter who dies mysteriously of nighttime fever, and Angela. She silently and viciously beats Angela after Bayardo returns her to the family home.

The Widower Xius: An old man. He has the misfortune to own the house that Angela wants to live in with Bayardo. Bayardo wears down the old man's resistance with offers of more and more money until Xius finally accepts an offer of ten thousand pesos. Xius's house sits on a windswept hill with a view of the Caribbean. Inside it he keeps treasured mementos of his long life with his beloved wife.

Reading
Chronicle of a
Death Foretold

🌱

Chapter 1

In the first sentence of the novel, **the narrator** tells us that **Santiago Nasar** will be killed. Early on a Monday morning, twenty-one-year-old Santiago rises from his bed. He left a wedding party celebration sometime around 4 A.M. This morning, his head aches and his tongue stings. The narrator says that he himself woke up after the wedding revelries in the lap of a woman. Just before Santiago woke this morning, he dreamed he was walking through a grove of timber trees. When he opened his eyes, however, he felt like he was covered with bird droppings.

The pale, slender young man changes into white linen clothes. Ordinarily he would put on khaki clothes and his boots, the clothes he wears to tend to the cattle ranch he inherited from his father, **Ibrahim Nasar**. As administrator of the ranch, he is also its protector, and he never leaves for the ranch without strapping on his powerful .357 Magnum. He keeps additional weapons in a closet and

WHITE MAN

Victoria Guzmán resentfully calls Santiago "white man," even though his skin is probably as dark as hers. Her slur shows her resentment. Santiago's father was an outsider, an Arab exploiter who became far wealthier than any of the local people who grew up in the small coastal village.

always sleeps with a Winchester rifle under his pillow, just as his father did before he died, three years earlier. Reaching for the Winchester, Santiago removes the bullets and puts them in a drawer of the night table, a lifelong habit. As a boy, Santiago saw a servant girl accidentally drop Ibrahim's Winchester, which discharged and ripped through the house next door before shattering a life-sized statue of a saint on the altar of a nearby church.

Santiago hurries through his mother's bedroom on his way to the bathroom. His mother, **Plácida Linero Nasar**, does not pay much attention when Santiago tells her about his strange dream. She discounts the trees and the bird droppings and makes a quick, simple analysis: the birds in Santiago's dream symbolize good health.

Plácida thinks of Santiago as a man so delicate and innocent that his skin chafed if she used starch in his clothes. Plácida asks Santiago about his unusual clothes, and he tells her that he dressed up "in pontifical style" just in case

> "The release of this literary work, so short and so widely publicized as a work of journalism, constitutes a unique event, without precedent in the history of publications in Latin America."
>
> **JOHN BENSON**

the bishop, who arrives by boat this morning, decided to visit the town. Plácida tells Santiago that the bishop will simply wave to the villagers, give the town a blessing, and disappear, as bishops always do. Still, Santiago hopes to see the bishop. He revels in church theatrics, which he likens to the movies. Santiago's mother reminds him to take an umbrella so that the chilly rain will not give him a cold. The narrator says that these are the last words Plácida speaks to her son.

Divina Flor Guzmán, the daughter of the Nasars' cook, **Victoria Guzmán**, is in the kitchen. Santiago comes in and Divina gives him a mug of mountain coffee laced with a shot of cane liquor, his usual Monday morning drink. Victoria thinks that Santiago looks unhappy. She and Divina hack up three rabbits for lunch, tossing the guts to the scrambling dogs.

Divina Flor, a young teenager, feels a rush of excitement when she sees Santiago gazing at her. When she walks over to collect his empty coffee mug, he seizes her wrist and tells her it is time she was "tamed." Victoria grabs a bloody knife and thrusts it toward Santiago, calling him "white man" and warning him that if he violates her daughter's purity, she will kill him. Years ago, Santiago's father seduced Victoria. For several years after that, they had sex in the stables.

LE DROIT DU SEIGNEUR
(THE MASTER'S RIGHT)

The feudal concept called *le droit du seigneur* gave the master of the house the right to have sex with any of his female servants. When the term *le droit du seigneur* was first used in 1825, it referred to the legal or custom-ary right of a feudal lord to have sexual  relations with a vassal's bride on her wed-ding night. Gradually, the term expanded to include a master's right to sleep with all female servants. García Márquez does not use this specific French term, but it is an apt description of the attitude the Nasar men take toward their servants. Ibrahim forced Victoria Guzmán to be his mistress, and Victoria fears that her daughter will become Santiago's sexual partner.

Eventually, old Nasar brought Victoria to the house to work as a servant. Another one of Victoria's lovers, not Nasar, fathered Divina Flor.

Santiago releases Divina's wrist and watches Victoria viciously wrench the guts from one of the freshly butchered rabbits. Repulsed, Santiago tells Victoria not to be so savage. Victoria pays no attention to him, flinging the entrails to the hungry dogs. Then they all hear the squawking horn of the bishop's steamboat.

The narrator pauses to tell us that the Santiago house used to be a warehouse two stories tall, with a tin roof on which buzzards used to roost. Many years ago, when Ibrahim Nasar arrived in town, he decided to use the old warehouse for an import-export business. He never did. Instead, he married and turned the warehouse into a home for his new bride. The home boasts a spiral staircase that leads upstairs to bedrooms. Plácida spent much of her time sitting alone on the balcony, looking with empty eyes at the almond trees in the town square.

The front door of the house, which leads to the town square, is always closed and barred. The narrator explains that Santiago will walk through this front door when he leaves the house on the day of his death. The narrator says that years after the murder, Victoria and Divina admitted that they knew of the murder plot by the time Santiago arrived in the kitchen that morning. Victoria said nothing because she secretly wanted Santiago to die.

Filled with hope and anticipation, Santiago hurries toward the door. Divina Flor runs before him, anxious to open the door for the young master of the house. Later, she tells the narrator that Santiago always tried to grope her when he had a chance, and before he left the house that morning, he "grabbed [her] whole pussy." It is early morning and still dark, and neither Divina Flor nor Santiago sees an envelope that was slipped under the door earlier, warning Santiago that he would be killed and explaining why. It is now 6 A.M.

Outside, the almond trees bloom, and scraps of wedding decorations litter the ground. Townspeople hurry toward the bishop's boat. **Pedro** and **Pablo Vicario**, the twin brothers who plan to kill Santiago, have been celebrating and drinking for three days and are still dressed in their formal wedding clothes. Asleep on benches in the milk shop, they awake when Santiago enters the square. The woman working at the milk shop knows of the Vicarios' plot. She sees Santiago dressed in white and later recalls that he "looked like a ghost."

As Plácida predicted, the bishop does not get off the steamboat. In fact, the boat does not even drop anchor, despite the sick people waiting for a blessing, the women carrying suckling pigs for the bishop, the piles of firewood for fuel awaiting donation, and the band striking up the bishop's anthem. As the boat chugs away, belching smoke, the bishop raises his hand like a mechanical puppet, making the sign of the cross again and again until the boat disappears from sight.

Gabriel García Márquez

Disappointed, Santiago turns to his friends **Cristo Bedoya** and Margot, who the narrator identifies as his sister. Santiago says he will change his clothes and join them in fifteen minutes at Margot's home. Margot envies the lovely **Flora Miguel**, whom Santiago has chosen to be his bride next Christmas. Margot urges Santiago to hurry, telling him that breakfast is already prepared. Santiago and Cristo head toward the town square. It is 6:25 A.M.

After the boat passes, Margot hears bits and pieces of gossip. **Angela Vicario**, the young woman whose marriage has been celebrated for the last three days with unending supplies of food and liquor, was returned to her father's house because her new husband discovered that she is not a virgin. Apparently, Angela's twin brothers, **Pedro** and **Pablo Vicario**, are bent on murderous vengeance.

Luisa Santiaga, the narrator's mother, seems to sense what is about to happen. When Margot tells her the gossip about the murder plot, Luisa goes to warn Plácida, Santiago's mother. As she runs toward the noisy town square, a man running in the opposite direction calls to her that Santiago is already dead.

UNDERSTANDING AND INTERPRETING
Chapter 1

Flashbacks: In cinematic fashion, García Márquez cuts back and forth between flashbacks and present tense, carefully building and relieving tension. The mystery of this novel is one of motivation and means, not of victim or criminal. The very first sentence of the novel reveals that Santiago will be killed. However, we still feel engaged and curious, for mystery surrounds the murder. The excitement of the narrative makes us think that we are reading about events taking place in the present tense, but when the tension builds, the narrator yanks us back, much like a movie camera pulling back, and reminds us with his asides that these events happened a long time ago.

A Self-Made Detective and a Murder Mystery: With this novel, García Márquez constructs a detective story and a psychological puzzle. The narrator, a self-fashioned detective, will talk to the villagers who remember the murder in an attempt to discover exactly what happened. The villagers will give him differing descriptions of the events. The reader must sift thought these contradictory accounts and try to decide who is telling the truth.

Many mysteries unfold. We wonder, for example, about Santiago's real character. Was he as his mother remembers, a man so delicate that starch hurt his skin and the butchering of rabbits disturbed him? Was he as Victoria remembers, simply "a shit" like his father, accustomed to slaughtering defenseless animals on his ranch? Was he as the narrator remembers, a merry, peaceful, openhearted man? We also wonder who knew that Santiago would be killed, and, similarly, who knew and did not do anything to stop the crime. We wonder why no one warned Santiago or his mother of his impending death. Finally, mystery surrounds the narrator himself. We wonder about his identity. We know that he was friends with Santiago, and we know a bit about his family, but he does not reveal himself fully.

Justifying Murder and Revenge: García Márquez asks us to consider hard questions about revenge. Revenge is at the center of most of our important myths and dramas, from Greek tragedies to *Beowulf* to Western movies. This novel raises questions about whether revenge, specifically murder, is ever justified. If a woman, and by extension her entire family, has been robbed of honor, perhaps only murder can heal the wound. Complicating this question is the fact that Santiago's small town has a specific code allowing revenge if a virgin is deflowered. Further complicating the question is the dubiousness of the charges against Santiago Nasar. No one knows if he actually took Angela's virginity, or if she willingly slept with him. It seems possible that he raped her, or that she is fantasizing, or even that she is lying outright. Every one of these scenarios is plausible, and every one changes the degree to which we can justify the revenge.

> " Asked why he showed the manuscript of *Chronicle of a Death Foretold* to Fidel Castro even before he submitted it to his publisher, García Márquez explained that Castro has 'a keen eye for spotting contradiction in a crime story like this.' "
>
> **ALFRED AND EMILY GLOSSBRENNER**

The Torture of Foreknowledge: *Chronicle of a Death Foretold* resembles a Greek tragedy in its agonizing affect on the audience. In both the novel and in Greek tragedies, we know what the inevitable and tragic conclusion will be, and we wince as we see how the tragedy could have been averted. These near-misses sting even though we know that the catastrophic conclusion is foregone. For example, Santiago's mother is a dream interpreter of some repute, but she fails to correctly interpret her son's dreams on the morning of his murder. Santiago senses the darkness of his dream, but his mother quickly dismisses the bad omens. In another painful moment, Santiago, who ordinarily dresses in khaki clothes, on Monday dresses all in white because of the bishop's visit. He looks like a sacrificial lamb in his white clothes, symbolic garb that seems to invite the twins to slay him. Santiago even receives a note warning of the impending murder, but he chances to miss seeing it. Although we know Santiago will die, it is painful to watch these small moments full of danger and foreshadowing, and to think that the tragedy could have been averted if only the characters could see what we see.

An Atmosphere of Violence: Suggestions of violence litter this chapter, beginning with the symbolism of Santiago's dream. He dreams that bird droppings will cover him, which foreshadows the blood that will cover him less than two hours after he awakens. Santiago's collection of high-powered guns also conjures up a grim atmosphere and shows that Santiago is familiar with killing. Santiago sleeps with a gun in his bed, which suggests his alertness to the possibility of a nighttime ambush. Victoria butchers rabbits with vigor and threatens Santiago with a knife. The threat of violent rape or at least sexual coercion lingers in the house. Various portents of death make Santiago's demise seem fated: When Santiago seizes Divina Flor's wrist, his hand feels like the "hand of a dead man" to her, and when the proprietress of the milk shop sees Santiago dressed all in white she thinks he "look[s] like a ghost."

> "The subject of *Chronicle of a Death Foretold* is the unthinkable. All of us will be mysteriously murdered, in the sense that we don't know why we must die. Any effort to explain or rationalize our fate—especially in the linearity of a chronicle—must collapse into the absurd."
>
> **LEONARD MICHAELS**

Chapter 2

After relating the basic story in the first chapter, the narrator pulls back and begins retelling the story from different angles, fleshing out the tale with flashbacks, hearsay, rumors, and gossip. The second chapter begins with a description of Bayardo's arrival in the village six months before the murder. People assume that Bayardo is gay because of his good looks and flashy, skintight clothes. However, Bayardo says he has come to town to find a bride. Bayardo soon wins the townspeople's admiration with his knowledge of engineering, railroads, Morse code, and frontier illnesses. He also plays cards expertly and can hold his liquor.

People say that Bayardo first sees Angela Vicario when she and her mother pass through the town square one August afternoon, dressed in black mourning clothes in memory of Angela's dead sister. Bayardo, only half-awake, spots the young woman and asks his landlady to remind him when he wakes that he plans to marry her.

A week or so later at a charity bazaar, Angela assists by calling out raffle winners. Bayardo buys all of the raffle tickets so that she will call out his name and reward him with the prize—a mother-of-pearl music box. He sends the music box to her later that night. Angela's parents and her hotheaded twin brothers assume that she was flirting with Bayardo at the bazaar. Despite the late hour, the brothers grab the music box and leave to return it to Bayardo. They return at dawn the next day, bringing Bayardo with them. The twins have been seduced by Bayardo's charm and his liquor.

Angela Vicario is the youngest daughter of a poor family. She was born with the umbilical cord wrapped around her neck—a sign of luck according to an old wives' tale that says all great queens are born that way. Angela's father, **Poncio Vicario**, was once a goldsmith renowned for his fine, intricate work, but he lost his vision as the result of this strenuous labor. Angela's mother, **Pura Vicario**, has given up everything in order to care for her family. Angela's two sisters married late. Another sister died of a mysterious nighttime fever. The twin boys have not yet married.

When the Vicario family hears the gossip that Bayardo intends to marry Angela, Pura demands that this stranger properly identify himself, which he does immediately. Bayardo's mother, father, and two sisters rattle into town in a Model T Ford. Most of the townspeople react worshipfully to Bayardo's father, General Petronio San Román, a legendary hero of the country's civil wars.

Unlike her family, Angela is not impressed with Bayardo, whom she hardly knows. However, her family says she cannot turn down this golden opportunity. Bayardo allows Angela to choose her future home, and she picks a farmhouse with a view of the Caribbean. The owner of the property initially refuses to sell, but caves in when Bayardo offers him ten thousand pesos in cash. The old, widowed landowner dies two months after selling the house.

It never occurs to anyone that Angela might not be a virgin. She has never dated anyone, and her mother watches her like a hawk. But Angela later confided to the narrator that during her engagement, she prayed for the courage to kill herself. Angela decides to tell her mother that she cannot marry Bayardo because she is not a virgin, but two of her friends talk her out of it, saying many new wives are not virgins. They tell Angela how to deceive her husband and secretly stain the sheets of the marital bed.

Bayardo wants the bishop to perform the ceremony, but Angela does not, for she objects to being married by a man who saves rooster combs for soup and throws away the rest of the fowl. Angela gets her way, but even without the bishop, the wedding is enormous and extravagant. Bayardo's sisters attend wearing butterfly wings attached to their dresses with golden brooches. None of the young men sense any change in Santiago's mood, and the narrator finds it hard to believe that Santiago could have masked his guilt so successfully if he had in fact slept with Angela.

Santiago guesses that the wedding cost nine thousand pesos, and Bayardo boasts that the sum is almost double Santiago's guess. The narrator tells us that he has confused memories of the wedding celebration, and other people's recollections are ragged. During the drinking and the feasting, the narrator proposed marriage to a girl who was still in primary school; he married her fourteen years later. The narrator vividly remembers Angela's blind father sitting in a seat of honor as drunken guests stumbled over him. The newlyweds appear in a new convertible, the groom shooting off sky rockets and drinking.

After the celebration, the narrator, his brother, Santiago, and Cristo Bedoya go to a whorehouse, or, as the narrator calls it, a "house of mercies." Angela's twin brothers are there, drinking and singing with Santiago. That night, knocking at the door wakens Angela's mother. It is Bayardo, who pushes Angela into the house. Angela's wedding dress is in shreds, and she has fastened a towel around her waist. Momentarily, Angela's mother thinks that her daughter is a ghost returned from the dead. Bayardo kisses the old woman's cheek and thanks her, calling her "mother" and telling her that she is a saint. Angela's mother silently beats her and then sends for the twins. Pedro demands to know "who it was." Angela looks away and names Santiago Nasar.

Chapter 2

Slippery Identities: It is hard to pin down the temperament of any character in this novel. García Márquez shows us that identity is a slippery beast. People can perceive the same man in almost opposite ways, and first impressions often prove untrustworthy. For example, when Bayardo San Román arrives by boat, the villagers assume his dashing good looks means he is gay. Later, however, Bayardo proves to be an almost exaggeratedly heterosexual man, arrogantly laying claim to a young woman he has never met and behaving with brash exuberance at his lavish wedding. No one quite agrees on the quality of Bayardo's character. The narrator's mother says Bayardo's eyes reminded her of the devil;

the narrator says Bayardo struck him as serious, good-mannered, and unusually sad, and that he seemed like clockwork wound too tightly; Angela is momentarily charmed by Bayardo when he sends her the mother-of-pearl music box, but soon turns against him. Bayardo seems conceited to some and decent to others.

Unreliable Memories: The narrator of this novel, and the people the narrator interviews, are untrustworthy. Even if they feel confident that they are telling the truth, and even if they earnestly relay what they remember, we cannot confidently trust their assertions. Memories fail and accounts contradict one another. For example, some villagers think that the weather on the day of the murder was brilliant and clear, but others remember that the weather was gloomy, and that rain fell as the murder took place. Three people who were in the boarding house when Bayardo impulsively decided to marry Angela swear Bayardo really fell for Angela in this instantaneous way. Four others who were in the boarding house are not sure. García Márquez suggests that it is impossible to come up with a perfectly factual account of a historical event, for even the most faithful accounts differ from one another, and memory is a flawed device.

Virginity and Machismo: In this small village, a family's honor matters above all else, and the premarital loss of a daughter's virginity inflicts a devastating blow to family honor. Virginity is a hallowed cult. An unmarried woman commits a grave sin by dishonoring herself and her family. Entwined with and central to this cult of virginity is the cult of *machismo*, a code that dictates male dominance over females, and male aggression toward weaker men. A man with machismo must take revenge on any man who robs his family of honor. Because they believe that Santiago took their sister's virginity, the twin Vicario sons have no choice but to punish him. Had they failed to do this, they would have debased the importance of virginity by implying that sex is not a crime punishable by death, and they would have called their own manhood into question by refusing to carry out their "duty." We know that the town accepts these precepts of machismo because many people knew of the plan to kill Santiago Nasar and did not warn him. With their silence, the townspeople show that they approve of the Vicario sons' crude justice.

A Touch of Magical Realism: This novel is objective and journalistic in tone, but occasionally García Márquez includes hints of the magical realism that features so prominently in his other novels. For example, Angela's sister dies mysteriously of nighttime fever, a vague, foreboding ailment. Bayardo's sisters attend the wedding wearing large, fantastical butterfly wings attached to their backs, which vividly illustrates the exoticism of Bayardo's family. The old widower reluctant to sell Bayardo his home of precious memories dies shortly after agreeing to sell. The doctor who puts his stethoscope to the widower's chest can hear "tears bubbling inside his heart." Impossible, of course—but these words make us ache with empathy for the old man. The fantastical touch affects more powerfully than would a factually accurate statement about the widower's cause of death. The fussy little bishop who sails by the village is known to be a connoisseur of well-fattened rooster combs, saving them for soup and throwing away what remains of the rooster. This almost unbelievable detail is a quick, effective way of showing the reader the bishop's character, and is far more colorful than spelling out the fact that the bishop is a spoiled sensualist and a corrupt dilettante.

Chapter 3

This chapter begins with an explanation of the legal defense the Vicario twins used during their trial. Their lawyer stated in court that they killed Santiago Nasar to defend the honor of the Vicario family, and therefore the killing was justified. The narrator then begins zigzagging back and forth in time, coming back to the night before the murder and then jumping forward to the morning of the murder, binding clues into a tighter story. Rather than following the narrator's backtracks and forward leaps, perhaps we can best understand the circumstances surrounding the murder if we look at a chronological sequence of events.

We hear the history of Santiago and **Mária Alejandrina Cervantes**, manager and employee at the whorehouse. At the age of fifteen, Santiago was so dazzled by Mária Alejandrina that his father banished him to the family ranch for a year. When Santiago returned to town, his lust had cooled, but he and Mária Alejandrina still cared for one another. If he were present in the whorehouse, Mária Alejandrina would refrain from sleeping with other clients for the sake of his feelings.

The Sunday night before the murder, Santiago, the narrator, the narrator's brother, and Cristo Bedoya visit the whorehouse. At 4 A.M, they go to the newlyweds' house to sing and set off rockets. The house stays dark. Even in the darkness of the night, they can see the eerie glow of Caribbean. Santiago jokes that the lights of a ship at sea might be the tormented soul of a slave trader. Because Santiago behaved so lightheartedly that night, the narrator cannot believe that guilt was plaguing him.

The men do not know it, but Bayardo has already returned Angela to her parents and now sits in the house alone. Santiago goes home to get a little sleep. It is the last time the narrator sees him. Santiago tells Victoria to send Divina Flor upstairs with some fresh clothes, but Victoria decides to bring them herself, wanting to keep her daughter away from "the claws of the seigneur."

When the Vicario brothers arrive home, they ask their sister who is responsible, and she names Santiago. Pablo is the older of the Vicario twins by six minutes, but it is Pedro who has always seemed more authoritarian. At twenty, Pablo stayed home and took care of the family, while Pedro served eleven months on the police force. Pedro returned with a venereal disease and a bullet wound that he enjoyed showing to friends. The rougher Pedro, according to his court confession, made the decision to kill Santiago.

The brothers go to the family pigsty and seize two knives. The butcher remembers that they sharpened the knives at the village meat market at 3:20 A.M., and Pablo boasted of their plan to kill

> " S ome years ago, I got into the car of Fidel Castro — who is a tenacious reader of literature — and on the seat I saw a small book bound in red leather. "It's my master Hemingway," Fidel Castro told me."
>
> **GABRIEL GARCÍA MÁRQUEZ**

Santiago Nasar. Pedro says that Santiago knows the reason why. At 4:10 A.M., the Vicario brothers go to the milk shop to buy some liquor and wait for Santiago. Pedro tells Clotilde Armenta, the proprietress of the milk store, that they are going to kill Santiago, adding that Santiago knows why. Clotilde remember that the twins looked "like two children." A beggar woman enters, and Clotilde asks her to warn Santiago's mother. The beggar woman leaves, and apparently, she does warn Victoria Guzmán.

A police officer sees the twins' knives and tells the mayor. Around 5 A.M., three other people tell the mayor about the murder plot. The mayor considers the Vicario twins "a pair of big bluffers," but he strolls to the milk shop and takes their knives away from them anyway. After the confiscation of the knives, Pedro feels his duty is finished, but the usually weaker Pablo disagrees. With difficulty, he convinces Pedro to return home for two more knives. At home, Pedro suffers painfully while trying to urinate, hugging a tree as he makes the attempt. Pablo finally puts a knife in Pedro's hand and drags him toward the town square.

By 6 A.M., news of the impending murder has spread throughout the town. The twins stop at the home of Pablo's fiancée, Prudencia, and talk with her mother, who has heard about their plan and seems sympathetic. The twins return to the milk store, where Clotilde gives them a bottle of "rotgut rum," hoping to get them too drunk to commit murder. Pedro borrows some shaving soap and begins shaving with his newly sharpened pig-butchering knife. Clotilde thinks he looks like a killer in the movies. Pablo shaves with a razor belonging to Clotilde's husband. Townspeople come in to buy unneeded milk just to take a look at the murderous twins.

> "This murder will stand among the many in modern literature as one of the most powerfully rendered."
>
> *THE NEW YORK TIMES*

The narrator's brother, Luis Enrique, has only clouded memories of what happened next, because of the liquor they had drunk during the night. Both Clotilde Armenta and the Vicario twins remember that the twins announced their plans to kill Santiago Nasar. The twins asked where Santiago was, and Luis Enrique said, "Santiago Nasar is dead," gave a blessing, and staggered out. Luis does not remember saying this. Later, Father Amador saw the Vicario twins cross the square but said nothing to them. At home, Luis woke from his sleep when one of his sisters ran into the bedroom crying out that Santiago Nasar had been killed.

UNDERSTANDING AND INTERPRETING
Chapter 3

A Pair of Harmless Murderers: Many townspeople hear that the Vicario twins plan to kill Santiago Nasar, but because the twins seem so harmless, few townspeople take their boast seriously, and therefore few do anything to impede them. The narrator says that because of the twins' excellent reputations, people dismissed their threat. One man comments that the gentle-hearted twins named their hogs after flowers instead of giving them human names. That way, they thought, butchering the hogs would not be quite so painful. Clotilde Armenta says that the twins looked "like two children." Colonel Lázaro Aponte took away their knives in a leisurely, unconcerned way, thinking them only "a pair of big bluffers."

A Dangerous Brand of Sex: In this novel, some sex is wonderful, and some sex is disastrous. There is the kind, companionable sex that goes on in the whorehouse, and there is the corrupting sex that infects and rips people apart. Pedro Vicario has experienced the same kind of destructive sex that his sister has suffered. We see the effects of this kind of sex when Pedro attempts to urinate, hugging a tamarind tree in an agony of pain, his penis infected and half-wrapped in a soiled bandage. Sex infects the Vicario twins' spirits, just as it infects their bodies. The illicit sex in which their sister engaged fills the twins with hatred that propels them toward murder.

Skewering the Bishop: García Márquez uses the bishop and the town priest to criticize the hypocrisy of some religious leaders and the blind devotion of the people who admire such leaders. The people deeply revere the bishop who occasionally passes by, and in tribute they bring him their fattest roosters and capons and immense stacks of firewood. He does nothing to merit this respect, however, and cares nothing for their sacrifices. He only floats by the village, slowly pumping his arm up and down in a mechanical blessing. The town priest is similarly dissatisfactory. Father Amador receives Clotilde Armenta's message about the Vicario twins' plan to kill Santiago, but he considers the threat a matter for the police to worry about. Furthermore, he worries more about catching a glimpse of the bishop than about protecting the life of a young man—a scandalous misplacement of energy for a priest.

Double Standards: In this novel, men and women follow entirely different sexual guidelines. Men frequent the town whorehouse whenever they want, and no one thinks twice about it. Santiago visits the whorehouse frequently, often with his friends, among them the Vicario boys and the narrator. In contrast, women in the town are categorized as either whores or saints. If a girl is not a whore, she must be a virgin saint. The cult of the Virgin Mary and the honor of the family, which rests partly on a daughter's virginity, are sacred. Male sexual fidelity, in contrast, matters to no one.

Chapter 4

Chapter 4 is less journalistic and objective in tone than the chapters that precede it. It uses satire, magical realism, and dark humor.

Santiago has been killed and an autopsy must be performed. The local doctor is not available, so Father Amador must do the slicing and dissecting, a duty he does not relish. Santiago's corpse lies in the Nasar living room, already putrid and fly-infested from the intense heat. In the kitchen, the family dogs howl, maddened by the smell of freshly butchered flesh. Santiago's mother shouts for someone to shoot the dogs, and soon someone obliges her.

The local druggist takes notes during the autopsy. Seven of the many wounds are defined as fatal. Father Amador discovers a golden holy medallion that Santiago swallowed as a child and a stab wound in the right hand that resembles a wound of the crucified Christ. Father Amador examines Santiago's brain and states that Santiago seemed to have superior intelligence and a brilliant future. However, after looking at the liver, he declares that Santiago probably had only a few years left to live. Later, the town doctor vehemently disagrees with Amador's diagnosis, saying that people in their part of the country always have large livers. Santiago's guts are pulled out and dumped into a garbage pail, and his body is stuffed with rags and quicklime and sewn up with twine before being placed inside a silk-lined coffin.

> "**M**árquez and his followers are sophisticated urban intellectuals who feign reverence for the simple wisdom of peasants."
>
> JONATHAN BATE

In the whorehouse, Mária Alejandrina wolfs down gargantuan platters of food to cope with her sorrow. The narrator goes to the whorehouse to mourn, but Mária Alejandrina drives him away, saying that he reeks of death and decay. Everything smells of Santiago's death. The rotting smell sickens the jailed Vicario twins. In addition, Pedro cannot urinate without suffering knifing pain, and Pablo has volcanic diarrhea. The matriarch of the small Arab community in town recommends an herbal potion that finally cures the twins' ailments.

The Vicario family packs up and leaves town forever, taking the disgraced Angela with them. She leaves in a bright red dress, her face concealed. Bayardo almost dies of alcohol poisoning, but he recovers and then continues drinking until his family arrives, hysterical and literally tearing their hair, to haul away his seemingly lifeless body.

Twenty-three years later, while the narrator is trying to make a living selling encyclopedias and medical books, he sees a woman sitting in a window. It is Angela Vicario, her hair yellowish gray, her once-beautiful eyes dim and spectacled. The narrator talks to Angela and discovers that she has become a mature and witty woman. Moreover, she proves quite willing to talk about her past, although she refuses to discuss key details, such as who really stole her virginity. The narrator believes that Santiago did not sleep with Angela, but Angela insists that it was indeed Santiago, saying "[h]e was the one." She chose not to stain her sheets on her wedding night because, she says, no one should be tricked like that, and besides, she felt ready to die.

Angela tells the narrator that after the murder, she saw Bayardo and went "crazy over him," thinking of him night and day, imagining that he was lying beside her in bed. She writes six letters to him over the course of six months, all of which go unanswered. The more letters she sends, the more her heart and body burn for him. For years, she writes a letter a week to Bayardo, some of them perfumed, some filled with furtive secrets, some businesslike, and some indignant. Sometimes she writes that she is ill, and even then she gets no letters. One day, an inkwell spills on her letter, and she scribbles that she is enclosing her tears. Seventeen years pass, and still no letter from Bayardo arrives.

One August day, someone raps on the door. It is Bayardo, now fat with thinning hair and bad eyesight. He carries a small suitcase containing a few clothes and a similar suitcase filled with Angela's letters, almost two thousand of them, arranged by date, tied up in ribbons, and all unopened.

UNDERSTANDING AND INTERPRETING
Chapter 4

After Murder, Panic: Gibbering chaos follows Santiago's murder. Only a few hours before the murder, the Nasar dogs greedily gobbled up the guts of the three rabbits that Victoria Guzmán was hacking up to prepare for lunch. Now those same dogs yap and jump, trying to get at Santiago's corpse and devour his guts, which someone inexpertly stuffed back under the slashes in his stomach. Almost operatically, Santiago's mother shouts for someone to shoot the dogs. There is no real need to shoot the dogs, who simply want food, but Mrs. Nasar's melodramatic reaction is characteristic of the panic that engulfs everyone after the murder. Everyone's nerves have been shattered, and the villagers behave irrationally and frenziedly.

Santiago as Christ Figure: Among other interpretations, it is possible to read Santiago as a Christ figure. Two signs in this chapter support such a reading: first, during the autopsy, Father Amador reaches into Santiago and discovers a holy medallion that Santiago swallowed as a child. Perhaps this literal token of goodness symbolizes the intangible goodness that Santiago carries inside himself like a medal. Further, the stab wound in Santiago's right hand resembles one of the wounds of the crucified Christ. Even if Santiago took Angela's virginity, the Vicarios make him a sacrificial lamb, just as Christ was. In order for the town to maintain its stability, it must uphold its code, and under the terms of that code, Santiago must die. Santiago's sexual experience does not undermine the Christ figure reading. Just as Santiago appreciates whores, Christ loved whores as he loved all people.

Poking Fun at the Mayor: García Márquez skewered the puffed-up, pretentious Father Amador in the previous chapter, and here he deflates the mayor with another satiric arrow. The mayor, a former state trooper, has to take charge of matters after Santiago's death, but he makes a comically gruesome mess of the business. He cannot think of anything helpful except to tell someone to keep Santiago's body refrigerated. This suggestion proves worthless, however, as no freezer in town is large enough to hold the corpse. Also, the mayor knows that the priest should not perform an autopsy, because the priest's medical knowledge is insufficient and the autopsy will not have legal standing, but he orders the priest to begin cutting nevertheless.

Less Journalism, More Magical Realism: In this chapter, García Márquez falls slightly away from the objective tone that has characterized the novel thus far and uses magical realism, the mode for which he is well known. He includes exaggerated, unlikely details and fantastical descriptions of people and events in order to vivify the narrative. Grotesque scenes of death are juxtaposed with gentle images. Spiritual elements mix with bizarre, secular language. The most persistent magical detail in this chapter is the putrefying smell of Santiago's slaughtered corpse, which flows through the town like blood. The smell will not come out of clothes even after they have been washed. The stench clogs up Pedro's innards and poisons Pablo's stomach. In the whorehouse, Mária Alejandrina eats and eats in an attempt to cope with her sorrow, and she sends the narrator away because he reeks of blood and grisly death.

Chapter 5

García Márquez begins this chapter with an elegiac tone that suggests a kind of epilogue. The narrator says that for years after the murder of Santiago Nasar, no one in the village speaks of anything else. For his part, the narrator spends years searching through mildewed files and official records, standing in water up to his ankles during the monsoon season, trying to learn about the legal case. The judge never finds anything to incriminate Santiago. Santiago seems to have been an innocent victim of the Vicario brothers, who wait three years in jail before they are tried and acquitted.

In court, Angela Vicario says only, "He [Santiago Nasar] was my perpetrator." During the three-day trial, she refuses to say anything more than this. Despite her insistence, however, Santiago's lawyer and his friends believe that Santiago was innocent. His friends say that Santiago's carefree behavior on the morning before his death proves that he did nothing wrong. If he had truly taken

Angela's virginity, he would have known that the price for his crime would likely be his life, and this knowledge would have affected his behavior. Yet, Santiago was far from worried. In fact, when he realized that the twins were going to kill him, he was bewildered.

The narrator thinks that perhaps the Vicario twins bragged about their plans because they hoped someone would stop them from killing Santiago, who was one of their best friends. They even told one of Santiago's best friends, Indalecio Pardo, what they were going to do. They must have been fairly sure that this friend would warn Santiago.

The narrator explains what happened on the day of Santiago's murder. By the time Santiago and Cristo Bedoya enter the town square, almost everyone there knows he will be killed, including the woman who owns the shoe store, an old man sitting in his pajamas, and Yamil Shaium, a fellow Arab and owner of a dry goods store. In fact, Yamil marvels at Santiago's good humor and says something about it to another Arab.

Cristo loses sight of Santiago and goes inside the Nasar home, where he tells Victoria that the twins plan to kill Santiago. She says the twins are too drunk to kill anyone. Cristo goes upstairs and takes Santiago's gun, not knowing that Santiago has emptied it of bullets. He leaves the house and sees the Vicario twins, pale and haggard, knives in their hands. They yell to him about what they plan to do. Cristo yells back, warning them that Santiago has a gun so powerful it can blow them to shreds. They do not believe him.

Cristo pleads with the mayor to do something. The mayor checks his social calendar to determine if he is scheduled to play dominoes that night. Desperately, Cristo runs to the narrator's house to see if Santiago is there. Santiago has gone to his fiancée's home, where she cries loudly, humiliated that everyone knows Santiago whored with Angela while engaged to her. She gives back all of Santiago's letters to her and says, "I hope they kill you!" Her family asks Santiago if he knows about the Vicario twins' plan for revenge. According to them, "he turn[s] pale" and seems confused by the news.

Santiago goes to the square, which is filled with people. Some of them shout to him not to go home, but when he turns to go another way, others shout for him to go yet another way. Then the Vicario twins spot him. They cross themselves and walk toward him. Santiago runs to his front door, but Plácida has barred it, thinking that Santiago is upstairs. Plácida hears terrible pounding on the door, and then she hears the thud of knives slicing deep into wood. At first there is no blood, so the twins stab harder and finally blood begins to flow. They keep knifing him, filled with rapture, ecstasy, and adrenaline, as if they are galloping on horseback.

THE NARRATOR UNMASKED

The novel almost finished, the narrator reveals that he is García Márquez, the author. He did not witness the murder of Santiago Nasar. He was lying in the lap of Mária Alejandrina when Santiago was killed. However, his aunt, Wenefrida Márquez, called to Santiago as he tottered toward his back door. She saw him gently wipe dirt from his exposed intestines.

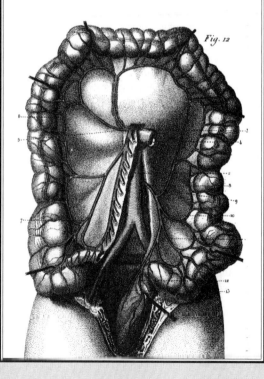

Fig. 12

The twins turn and run to the church to confess. Santiago staggers up, trying to hold in his guts. He totters unsteadily to the house next door, where Poncho Lanao and his wife and children are sitting down to breakfast. Poncho Lanao remembers the overwhelming "smell of shit." The oldest daughter remembers that Santiago, with his dark curls, looked more handsome than ever. The narrator's aunt shouts to Santiago, and he answers that he has been killed. He stumbles, gets up, brushes the dirt off his exposed guts, enters his own house, and falls face down in the kitchen.

UNDERSTANDING AND INTERPRETING
Chapter 5

"Lagoon of lost causes": García Márquez uses his hallmark style to describe the Palace of Justice in Riohacha, where the narrator examines legal records of the trial of the Vicario brothers. García Márquez tells us that the building is very old. In fact, the sixteenth-century explorer Sir Frances Drake used it for his headquarters for two days. During high tide, while the narrator searches for more files, the ground floor floods, and he works in water up to his knees in this "lagoon of lost causes." This fantastical account of the narrator's work suggests his loneliness and the futility of looking for explanations.

Bayardo's Sexual Orientation: We never find out whether Bayardo is gay or straight. Some signs seems to confirm the townspeople's original assumption that Bayardo is homosexual. The townspeople make this assumption because when Bayardo moves to town, he is too slender, too good-looking, and too provocatively dressed. Yet when he begins talking about "manly" matters and when he spies Angela Vicario and instantly decides to marry her, they decide he is straight. Still, Bayardo never visits María Alejandrina's whorehouse, as most of the other men do, nor does he ever court Angela. We have no idea what happens in the bedroom between him and Angela after the wedding. The village assumes that he returns her because she is not a virgin, but Bayardo says nothing about her virginity when he goes to her parents' house. It begins to seem possible that the townspeople's first interpretation of Bayardo was the correct one. Bayardo goes on to drink himself into such terrible alcoholic stupors that he is more dead than alive when his family comes for him. He never marries, he grows fat, and he does not bother to read any of Angela's letters. We never really discover whether it was anger at his new wife or shame at his own sexuality that causes Bayardo to return Angela to her parents' home.

BITTER PEPPER CRESS SEEDS

Pepper cress seeds are harvested from watercress, a bitter, pungent green plant that grows in fresh-running ponds. The seeds are extremely caustic when bitten. By chewing them incessantly, Plácida Linero subjects her tongue to perpetual pain in order to punish herself for failing to prevent her son's murder.

Nasturtium officinale

Gabriel García Márquez

Painful Irony: One of the most painful ironies in the novel involves Santiago's mother. Although renowned as an interpreter of dreams, she discerns nothing ominous in Santiago's dream on the morning of the murder. That dream ends with Santiago spattered with bird feces, an image that resonates during the murder. The father of Santiago's fiancée remembers that moments before Santiago was killed, he "looked like a wet little bird." When Santiago staggers into the his neighbors' house, there is a "terrible smell of shit." The degree to which life imitates the dream suggests that the murder could have been averted had Plácida correctly interpreted her son's dream. After Santiago's murder, she lies slothfully in her hammock, staring into space, unable to forgive herself, chewing pepper cress seeds.

Autopsy of a Death: In one sense, the narrator of the novel performs an autopsy, just as the priest does. García Márquez attempts to piece together the story of the murder, examining diverse memories, weather reports, gossip, hearsay, rumors, characters, the bright-spangled mood of celebration, and the dark, funeral ironies. He performs an autopsy on individual memories, communal memories, and court records. Just as Amador slices through Santiago's liver, the narrator slices through old memories, trying to get at the core of what took place. Just as Father Amador looks into Santiago's brain, the narrator looks into the Vicario brothers' penchant for butchery, the cult of a virgin's honor, and the cult of machismo. He looks for the truth, the logic that could explain the unhappy murder.

The Sacrificial Lamb: Dressed in white linen, slashed by pig-butchering knives, Santiago serves a sacrificial lamb to the community's code of honor. There is no proof that he has taken the virginity of Angela Vicario, but because she names Santiago as her perpetrator, it falls to him to be sacrificed. Many elements of Santiago's murder suggest a pagan sacrifice. An archetypal sacrifice is often performed during a celebration such as the gala three-day wedding in this novel. Parties, gaily-colored decorations, excess drinking, and voracious eating make up the spectacle surrounding the sacrifice. The crowd stands around the village square, prepared to watch the slaughter that they all know is about to happen. No one does anything to stop it. When the murder takes place, Santiago, the innocent lamb, does not bleed. Three times the knives pierce him, and three times the brothers pull them back bloodless.

Along with its similarities to pagan sacrifice, Santiago's murder recalls the crucifixion of Jesus Christ. Santiago's family name, Nasar, suggests Nazareth, the region of Jesus' birth. The narrator describes the wound in Santiago's hand as resembling the wound in Christ's hand. When the Vicario brothers finish killing Santiago, they rush off to the church to confess. What the crowd has witnessed is shocking, frightening, abhorrent, and hideous—and yet no one turns away. Like characters in a Greek tragedy, the townspeople know beforehand what will happen and thus become co-conspirators in the death that is needed to sustain and strengthen the village code of honor.

Conclusions

The novel ends without final solutions and without a definition of justice. We are given village speculations, embroidered recollections, faded memories, contradictory weather reports, old dreams, fragments of letters, and half-truths —none of which add up to make a tidy moral. García Márquez wants us to consider who is to blame for the killing. The townspeople? They know that this murder will happen, and yet they do nothing. Some of them approve of the planned slaughter. They stand on the sidelines, their eyes riveted on the victim in the killing arena.

Are the twins solely to blame? The twins have been raised, in typical fashion, to be men and to have machismo. According to the moral law of the town, they have almost no choice but to kill Santiago for defiling their sister. And yet they carry out this duty with extreme reluctance. They tell everyone about their plans, as though they want to be prevented from carrying them out. These young men, experts at carving up pigs, kill Santiago like amateurs. The repugnance with which they kill Santiago suggests that the town's codes cause the murder, not the twins' bloodthirst. The twins commit the murder on their own, but they are also enacting the general will of the townspeople by slaughtering Santiago.

The murder seems not only foretold, but predestined. In a small town built on a foundation of repression of its women, arrogant patriarchy, and a sacred code of revenge, justice adds up to the exchange of one murdered man for one defiled virgin.

IV

LOVE
IN THE TIME
OF CHOLERA

Love in the Time of Cholera

An Overview

🌿

Key Facts

Genre: Comic epic; magical realistic novel

Date of First Publication: *El Amor en Los Tiempos del Cólera*, 1985 (trans. *Love in the Time of Cholera*, 1988)

Setting: Around 1875–1930 in a seaport city on the northern coast of Colombia, South America

Narrator: Anonymous, third-person omniscient (all-knowing)

Plot Overview: Florentino Ariza falls desperately in love with young Fermina Daza and swears everlasting love to her. She spurns him and eventually marries the rich, good-looking Dr. Juvenal Urbino. The novel follows Florentino Ariza, Dr. Urbino, and Fermina Daza through the next fifty-some years as they live through Colombia's difficult transition from a country of banana plantations to a country of the industrial twentieth century.

Style, Technique, and Language

Style—A Surprise Death: *Love in the Time of Cholera*, as its title suggests, deals with love and death, often in unconventional ways. The first chapter begins with the death of a close friend of Dr. Juvenal Urbino's and ends with the surprising

Gabriel García Márquez

death of Dr. Urbino himself. García Márquez has told us about Dr. Urbino's youth, his father's career as a physician, his marriage, and his humorous quirks, so it comes as a shock when Urbino dies. As readers, we have been trained to expect that characters to whom the author devotes time and energy will not be killed off in the first chapter. García Márquez flouts these expectations. The element of surprise is one of García Márquez's stylistic aces, but it is more than a gimmick. It is a way of making fiction resemble life, in which death strikes not just minor characters, but people we know and love.

> "There's nothing deliberate or predictable...nor do I know what's going to happen in my fiction. I'm at the mercy of my imagination."
>
> **GABRIEL GARCÍA MÁRQUEZ**

The first chapter's concentration on Dr. Urbino provides a context for one of the novel's climactic events of love: Florentino Ariza's declaration of everlasting love and fidelity to Urbino's widow.

Technique—Picaresque Sexual Adventures: The structure of *Love in the Time of Cholera* resembles the structure of Miguel Cervantes's masterpiece, *Don Quixote*. Like the idealistic knight Don Quixote, Florentino Ariza is an idealist who longs for a woman he does not know well. When Florentino Ariza's beloved Fermina Daza rejects his proposal of marriage, he vows that someday he *will* marry her. Dr. Urbino, the husband of her choice, *will* die eventually. Florentino Ariza will wait, and he does. But during that fifty-year-long wait, he becomes one of the most extravagantly successful lovers in literature, bedding women easily and gluttonously. *Don Quixote* chronicles the **picaresque** adventures of its hero, and *Love in the Time of Cholera* chronicles the picaresque lovemaking adventures of Florentino Ariza. These adventures are described with fantasy, madness, and whimsy—narrative ingredients that enable García Márquez to **satirize** the cliché of the so-called Latin lover. For instance, unbeknownst to the very heterosexual Florentino Ariza, most people think that he is a homosexual.

Language—Magical Realism: *Love in the Time of Cholera*, like many of García Márquez's novels, features magical realism. For instance, Florentino Ariza shows up immediately after Urbino's funeral to declare his love to Urbino's grieving widow. In real life, it is unlikely that an old suitor would seek out a former lover immediately following the funeral of her husband, but in García Márquez's fiction, this almost unbelievable move simply emphasizes the urgency of Ariza's love for Fermina Daza.

Characters in
Love in the Time of Cholera

Florentino Ariza: The man who becomes hopelessly smitten with young Fermina Daza when he is only ten years old. Florentino Ariza is mostly misunderstood during his long life—ridiculed for his melodramatic romanticism, labeled a homosexual, and, because of his heavy black clothes, sad eyes, and shaggy dark hair, pitied by women, who attempt to nurture him with sex and strong mountain coffee.

Leona Cassiani: A young, pretty black woman. Florentino Ariza is attracted to her, but thinks she is a whore, a problem because Florentino has taken a pledge never to pay for sex. Nonetheless they become platonic friends, and eventually Florentino Ariza convinces his Uncle Leo XII to offer Leona a menial job. Leona impresses Uncle Leo XII so much that he makes her his executive secretary. Leona, eternally grateful for Florentino Ariza's generosity, mothers him when he gets old.

Lorenzo Daza: A mule trader and the obese father of Fermina Daza. He desperately wants Fermina to marry well and reacts with fury when her academy expels her for writing a love letter to Florentino Ariza during one of her classes. After discovering hundreds of Florentino Ariza's love letters to Fermina, Lorenzo takes her on a long journey to visit relatives, hoping that she will forget about the poet.

Jeremiah de Sainte-Amour: A longtime friend of Urbino, he commits suicide at the age of sixty and dies on the army cot that he slept on as a soldier, his Great Dane dying beside him. Jeremiah came to the city long ago as a refugee, bringing a secret lover with him, a woman unknown even to Urbino. Eventually, Jeremiah gained a reputation as a perceptive photographer of children.

Uncle Leo XII Loayza: Florentino's uncle. One of García Márquez's most delightful eccentrics, Uncle Leo XII engineers the economic prosperity of his company, the River Company of the Caribbean. After all of Uncle Leo XII's sons die quirky deaths and his daughters resettle along New York's Hudson River, he reluctantly begins grooming Florentino Ariza as his heir. His fondest wish is to sing opera arias so perfect and beautiful that they shatter expensive, centuries-old Chinese vases.

Sara Noriega: Blessed with luminous, mother-of-pearl skin and plump contours, Sara takes pity on Florentino Ariza when his poem fails to win the Golden Orchid award at the Poetic Festival. She takes him home for solace and soon becomes his sexual partner. Sara collects baby pacifiers and hangs them from her headboard to suck on during sex.

Rosalba: A mysterious woman traveling on the boat that bore Florentino Ariza toward the Andes. Traveling with two other women and an infant in a bird cage, Rosalba drags Florentino Ariza into her cabin one night and takes his virginity.

> "García Márquez has extraordinary strengths and firmness of imagination and writes with the calmness of a man who knows exactly what wonders he can perform."
>
> **ALFRED KAZIN**

Hildebranda Sánchez: Fermina Daza's cousin. Hildebranda welcomes the weary Fermina Daza after her long journey. Herself a victim of fiery, reckless love, Hildebranda recognizes a kindred spirit in Fermina Daza.

Fermina Daza Urbino: As a young girl, Fermina Daza lives with her father and his sister in the ruins of an old house. Her aunt becomes Fermina Daza's confidante when Fermina falls in love with the forlorn Florentino Ariza. When Fermina Daza reaches the age of twenty-one, she surrenders to Juvenal Urbino's entreaties and agrees to marry him. After Fermina is widowed, she finally discovers the delights of good sex.

Dr. Juvenal Urbino: After spending several years in Paris and graduating from medical school, Urbino returns to his provincial home on the Colombian seacoast, fired with hope and ambition. He plans to eradicate cholera, oversee progressive sanitation measures, and foster good music, literature, and theater in his decaying city. Urbino achieves many of these goals.

Reading
Love in the
Time of Cholera

Chapter 1

One day, when eighty-one-year-old **Dr. Juvenal Urbino** answers an urgent call, he finds the corpse of his old friend **Jeremiah de Saint-Amour** covered with a blanket and lying on an army cot. Beside Jeremiah lies his black Great Dane, also dead. Urbino smells cyanide, which smells like bitter almonds, and concludes that Jeremiah killed himself.

Clutter fills Jeremiah's apartment, but everything is carefully dusted. A young intern, who was also summoned, wants to perform an autopsy and see firsthand what cyanide does to a corpse, but Urbino tells the intern that he will have many years to see the results of cyanide, which is the usual answer for defeated love. Urbino tells a police officer that Jeremiah, acclaimed photographer of children, died of natural causes. Urbino arranges for the burial, saying he will pay all expenses.

Dr. Urbino strictly adheres to daily schedules, and he does not easily tolerate interruptions to his agendas. It pains him that he is missing High Mass on Pentecost Day, an important day of worship in the Roman Catholic church. Urbino notes Jeremiah's unfinished chess game and then opens a thick envelope that the inspector hands him. Inside are eleven pages in Jeremiah's careful handwriting. Urbino tries to disguise his unhappiness and discomfort as he reads the letter. He worries about this loss of time, for he absolutely must appear at a luncheon that

THE LIBERATOR

Throughout the novel, García Márquez places references to statues of The Liberator —some statues almost hidden by trees, some crumbling—as well as references to the shrine where he died. The Liberator in question is Simón Bolívar (1783–1830), one of South America's greatest generals, whose armies drove out the Spanish colonists and liberated five South American republics. Often referred to as the George Washington of South America, Bolívar served as president of Colombia from 1819 to 1828.

day celebrating Dr. Olivella's fifty years as a physician. He must also take the time to go see the woman about whom Jeremiah wrote in his last confession.

Urbino goes in his horse-drawn carriage to an unnumbered house. A haughty, golden-eyed mixed-race woman opens the door. She is around forty years old. For years, she tended to Jeremiah devotedly, and she was with him until a few hours before his death. They were secret lovers ever since they met in a convalescent home in Haiti. She was Jeremiah's opponent in his last, unfinished chess game. During this game, she realized that Jeremiah was moving "his pieces without love." Years ago, she tells Urbino, she and Jeremiah were lying naked together on a beach when he decided that he would commit suicide at the age of sixty. She objected to Jeremiah's decision to kill the dog with cyanide fumes, so she tied a slipknot around the dog's throat so that he could escape. Apparently, the dog chose to die alongside Jeremiah. Urbino does not like the woman. It seems obvious to him that she will never observe proper mourning. He thinks she will probably sell Jeremiah's house and continue living in the slums.

> "Had Bolívar not existed, Mr. García Márquez would have had to invent him."
>
> **MARGARET ATWOOD**

The narrator tells us that Urbino has lived in Europe and his mansion is furnished with treasures from France, Austria, Spain, and Turkey. At one time, the mansion was filled with a menagerie of mastiffs, dogs, cats, a monkey, and even a giant anaconda that fed on bats and salamanders. Then, one of the mastiffs went mad and began killing every animal in sight. After that disaster, Urbino declared that anything unable to speak could never enter the house. Following the letter of this rule but not the spirit, Urbino's clever wife, **Fermina Daza**, bought him an extraordinary talking parrot. Urbino teaches the parrot academic French and Italian arias. Unfortunately, three hours ago, the parrot escaped from a servant who was clipping his wings, and a fire brigade was called to help capture the bird.

Fermina Daza, seventy-two years old, urges her husband to hurry to get ready for the luncheon. She bathes him, lays out his clothes, and dresses him. She has been married to Urbino for many years, during which time she has been neither very happy nor very unhappy. The couple almost divorced once after arguing about whether or not Fermina Daza had remembered to put a fresh bar of soap in the bathroom. This morning, Fermina Daza does not want her husband's somber mood to infect her good one. So what if old Jeremiah died, leaving behind a hidden lover? Why should that disturb anyone? So what if Jeremiah kept his corrupt past a secret until writing one last letter? Some things are best kept secret.

At the luncheon, 120 guests feast on rare and exotic food. They prepare to eat chickens whose gizzards often yield tiny nuggets of gold. Precisely at noon, a bolt of lightning slams into the earth. Rain falls, uprooting trees, turning the festive patio into a quagmire, and driving the guests inside. Dr. Urbino continues to fret about the disturbing secrets Jeremiah kept from him. Fermina Daza pats his hand.

Several guests have heard of Jeremiah's death and want details, commenting on people who commit suicide because of love. Urbino's son arrives with dessert for everyone, but Urbino leaves almost immediately. He wonders if he has time for his scheduled siesta. At home, Urbino's servants are still attempting to capture the elusive parrot. Urbino naps in a bedroom that has been mostly destroyed by the firemen and their power hoses. When he awakens, he decides to catch the parrot himself. Slowly climbing a ladder, Urbino momentarily grasps the parrot by the throat. Then the ladder slips, and Urbino falls to his death on the muddy tiles below.

At Urbino's funeral, Fermina Daza slips off her wedding ring and puts it on her husband's finger, assuring him that they will see each other soon. Among the few people who stay after the funeral is seventy-six-year-old **Florentino Ariza**, with an old-fashioned mustache waxed at the tips, a shining bald head, and dark mourning clothes. Once alone with Fermina Daza, he places his hat over his heart and says he has waited more than fifty years to repeat to her his vow of eternal love. Utterly confused, Fermina Daza orders him out and slowly bars the door. She goes up to bed. In the morning, she realizes that while she slept, she thought more about Florentino Ariza than about her dead husband.

UNDERSTANDING AND INTERPRETING
Chapter 1

Many Shades of Love: We see many varieties of love in this chapter. Dr. Juvenal Urbino has seen many cases of unrequited love. An old and cynical man, he has handled plenty of suicides, victims of unrequited love who have killed themselves by inhaling cyanide fumes. Jeremiah has a secret, illicit love of which he does not speak until the day of his death. Urbino has loved Jeremiah for many years with the affectionate love of a friend. In order to preserve Jeremiah's reputation, Urbino insists that Jeremiah's death be officially recorded as a natural one, not a suicide. Fermina Daza feels longtime marital love for

Urbino, a love more protective than passionate. She almost mothers him, bathing him and dressing him. They have been married for fifty years and depend on each another. They never speak of their love. Florentino Ariza feels impassioned, sworn love for Fermina Daza, despite her decision, fifty years earlier, to marry the young, promising Dr. Juvenal Urbino. So long-lasting is Florentino Ariza's love that he comes back to proclaim it to Fermina Daza mere hours after the death of her husband.

More prosaic kinds of love exist in this chapter, too. Jeremiah's dog exhibits the love of a pet for its master. Although the dog could have escaped the cyanide fumes, it chose to stay with Jeremiah, keeping him company even in death. Urbino exhibits a human's love for his pet. He loves his parrot extravagantly, investing hundreds of hours in teaching it academic French and European operatic arias. In one sense, Urbino dies for his parrot, for he dies while trying to capture it. Urbino, Jeremiah, and Jeremiah's secret lover love the game of chess, which has symbolic value: during Jeremiah's last game, his lover realized that Jeremiah was moving "his pieces without love," a sign of his impending suicide. Urbino loves routine. For years, he has lived according to rigid schedules. Punctuality and regularity define him, and he feels nervous when he must deviate from his plans.

> "It could be argued that this is the only honest way to write about love, that without the darkness and the finitude there might be romance, erotica, social comedy, soap opera—all genres, by the way, that are well represented in this novel—but not the Big L."
>
> **THOMAS PYNCHON**

Magical Touches: García Márquez fills this first chapter with fantastical flourishes. Sprinkled among the commonplace, the ordinary, and the banal events of everyday living, we get over-the-top, lavish, imaginative details. The color gold appears repeatedly, in the gold cyanide, chickens with tiny gold nuggets in their gizzards, and the "cruel, golden eyes" of Jeremiah's secret lover. Urbino says that suicides involving cyanide fumes always have "crystals in their heart." García Márquez juxtaposes the joyful photographs on Jeremiah's walls, which feature children celebrating communion, birthdays, and holidays, with the stiff, blue corpse of the man who captured these jubilant moments. García Márquez hovers over Urbino's horse-drawn carriage, delighting in its incongruity (no one uses horse-drawn carriages anymore), and pointing out the anachronistic top hat and velvet uniform of Urbino's coachman as the coach navigates the narrow, foul, littered streets of the slums to ferret out Jeremiah's secret lover. Of Jeremiah's secret lover, García Márquez says she will probably spend the rest of her life "simmering" while sinister storms and summer winds tear roofs off houses and carry children away through the air. This is fortissimo magical realism, as is the mention of the Spanish galleon, lying just outside the harbor, entombed with casks of precious jewels and gold worth 500 billion pesos.

Urbino's parrot strikes the high note of magical realism. The parrot can trill arias in a voice that rivals the voices of the best divas in Europe, and it can abruptly darken its voice to become a wooing Italian tenor. It can even recite the Mass in Latin. Of course, no parrot can do this, but we believe that this one can. We suspend disbelief, just as we do when we hear about the destruction of Urbino's house—furniture slashed, portraits destroyed, trees stripped, and rugs ruined—in an attempt by the firemen and their power hoses to try to capture this remarkable parrot, for whom Urbino literally dies.

Chapter 2

At the age of ten, Florentino Ariza must quit school and help his mother make a living. Florentino Ariza's father does not acknowledge him. Florentino Ariza finds work in the Postal Agency doing menial tasks. The young girls have secret bets about which one of them Florentino Ariza will choose as his wife. One day, when Florentino Ariza delivers a telegram to the home of **Lorenzo Daza**, he spies the beautiful, almond-eyed Fermina Daza giving reading lessons to her aunt. She is about his own age. Florentino Ariza falls instantly in love with her. He smells the garland of fresh gardenias she wears, and associates that smell with her for the rest of her life.

Florentino Ariza begins shadowing Fermina Daza as she walks to school and church with her aunt. He starts writing what will eventually become a seventy-page letter to Fermina. He confesses his fervent love for Fermina Daza to his mother, who says he must first win over Fermina's aunt before trying to win Fermina. What Florentino Ariza does not know is that Fermina Daza glanced up from her reading lesson just as Florentino Ariza was walking down the hallway in her home. His bespectacled, forlorn look impressed her, and she noticed when he began watching her. Before long, Fermina Daza's aunt begins to recognize Florentino Ariza as the ever-present, woeful boy dressed in black and pretending to read. She predicts that someday he will give Fermina Daza a love letter.

Months pass, and one day when Fermina Daza's aunt goes inside, Florentino Ariza asks Fermina Daza to accept a letter from him. She tells him that she must ask her father's permission. Days later, on seeing the agreed-upon signal, Florentino Ariza hands her a half-page of confession, promising fidelity and everlasting devotion. Bird droppings spatter Fermina Daza's white embroidery cloth. Florentino Ariza becomes infected by a threatening case of love sickness for Fermina Daza. His mother nurses him, gravely noting his fever, green vomit, and diarrhea. She knows that the symptoms of love duplicate the symptoms of cholera.

Florentino Ariza's lovesickness makes him lackadaisical and begins to cause chaos at the Postal Agency, so his boss arranges for him to have a private room in a

> " I'm delighted not only with his work but with the influence he's had on other writers. He's done so much for putting the lavish imagination back into prose; younger writers aren't quite so afraid of swimming freely."
>
> **ROBIE MACAULEY**

nearby whorehouse, where he can read, write poetry, and pine away for his beloved. This boss has miniscule genitals, like those on the pink cherubs in the Cathedral. However, because he massages his genitals with a secret snake venom ointment, he has become a sexual legend at the local brothel.

Florentino Ariza and Fermina Daza write to each other, sometimes as often as twice a day. Fermina Daza's aunt ensures that Fermina Daza's father does not discover the exchange of letters. Two years pass, and Florentino Ariza writes a formal proposal of marriage to Fermina, whose aunt advises her to accept. Fermina Daza writes to Florentino Ariza that she will marry him as long as he never makes her eat eggplant.

Florentino Ariza's mother and Fermina Daza's aunt both advise the two young lovers to wait two years before speaking further of marriage, which they do. The love of Fermina Daza changes Florentino Ariza. He grows confident and begins buying books of exquisite Castilian poetry to read in his little whorehouse cubicle. He frolics with the naked whores, sharing food and jokes. He is never tempted to sleep with them because of his reverence for Fermina Daza.

Four months before the official engagement is to be finalized, Lorenzo Daza walks into the Postal Agency and asks to speak to Florentino Ariza alone. Fermina has been expelled from school for writing a love letter to Florentino, and Lorenzo searched until he found hundreds of packets of Florentino Ariza's letters. Because

THE BLOODSTAINED MACHETE

Although Colombia was liberated from Spanish colonialism in 1820 by Simón Bolívar, it rarely enjoyed peace. The country was continually at war, with the Liberals fighting against the Conservatives in guerrilla raids and small, poorly organized armies. Conservatives had headquarters inland, mostly in the hills. The balance of power swung back and forth. For a while, the Conservatives would hold political sway, only to be toppled a few years later by Liberals, who ruled for a few years, until the swing of the bloodstained machete reversed its course again. All told, more than a hundred thousand people died over the course of these nineteenth-century wars.

his sister helped conceal this illicit romance, Lorenzo shipped her off on a schooner. As for Fermina Daza, Lorenzo will make sure that someday she becomes a grand lady in a "fortunate marriage." Lorenzo snarls at Florentino to get out of the way. Florentino Ariza does not frighten easily. Even when Lorenzo threatens to shoot him, he says there is no better way to die than "to die for love."

The next month, Lorenzo and his daughter leave the city, traveling for weeks with a caravan of mule drivers along the dangerous ridges of the Andes. They camp in Indian settlements while a civil war rages around them. The sour, urine-stained, rented canvas cots repulse Fermina. They finally descend into the valley where Fermina Daza's maternal uncle lives. One of Fermina Daza's cousins, **Hildebranda Sánchez**, bathes the blisters that have risen on Fermina Daza's buttocks after her long ride astride a donkey. That night, Hildebranda gives Fermina an envelope permeated with the scent of white gardenias. Inside are eleven telegrams from Florentino. Lorenzo Daza made a mistake by telegraphing his in-laws to tell them of his journey. He forgot that Florentino Ariza works in the telegraph office. With the help of other young men working in outlying telegraph offices, Florentino Ariza has kept track of the Dazas.

Lorenzo and his daughter return to the city by boat, making a perilous landing. Fermina Daza is so drenched that Florentino Ariza cannot recognize her from his hiding place. At home, in a formal ceremony, Lorenzo gives his daughter responsibility for the house. She is seventeen now.

Florentino Ariza finally sees Fermina Daza again in the marketplace. He watches her confidently ignore the snake charmers, the beggars, and the disreputable vendors. Fired with a new independence, she samples sausages, crushes sage and oregano, and dabs French perfume behind her ear. She buys yards of linen for the dining room table that she and Florentino Ariza will have, lengths of percale for their wedding sheets, and a bottle of gold ink.

Florentino Ariza says, "This is not the place for a crowned goddess." Fermina turns and looks at his trembling face and fearful, empty eyes, and she instantly decides that she has been wasting her time idealizing this pathetic young man. She waves him away, saying "[f]orget it." She returns all of his letters and asks that he return all of hers. Florentino Ariza must obey. He returns everything except a long, thick braid of her hair that she sent to him. Florentino Ariza's mother is forced to return that herself.

UNDERSTANDING AND INTERPRETING

Chapter 2

Secret Upon Secret: Florentino Ariza's vow of secret love to Fermina Daza and their mutual agreement to a secret engagement form the centerpiece of the novel, and many other secrets surround that central secret. Jeremiah has had a secret lover for many years. Urbino is fastidious about his secret rituals of hourly pill taking. Because of Urbino's stature as the city's most prestigious doctor, people respect his decision to keep Jeremiah's suicide secret. Don Pius V Loayza, Florentino Ariza's biological father, never acknowledges Florentino Ariza as his son, and insists on keeping his payment of Florentino Ariza's expenses a secret. The girls hold secret lotteries about which one of them Florentino Ariza will choose as his sweetheart and wife. Florentino Ariza first sees Fermina Daza in her role as her aunt's secret reading instructor. When he falls in love with her, he begins his "secret life as a solitary hunter," watching Fermina as she and her aunt pass a small park four times on weekdays and once on Sundays. Florentino Ariza writes many secret letters to Fermina Daza before he finally summons the courage to give one to her. Later, Fermina Daza reads that first letter over and over, hoping to find a secret code. Florentino Ariza's mother has a secret lover and a secret horde of gold hidden in a clay pot under her bed. During the course of the novel, all of these secrets will be revealed, and as they come to light, they change lives.

> "García Márquez's winning the Nobel Prize for Literature is very important because it breaks open the Anglo-Saxon notion of what the novel genre is all about."
>
> JUSTIN KAPLAN

A City in Progress: One of García Márquez's central themes in *Love in the Time of Cholera* is the effect of progress on this small, anonymous city on the Caribbean seacoast. He is interested in how the city has slowly adapted to scientific discoveries, new modes of transportation, and modern values. In Chapter 1, Dr. Juvenal Urbino expressed just pride in having established new innovations in the sanitary conditions of the bay area. He did not always succeed, but he always tried hard. In this chapter, we see how the social elite of the city have been forced to adapt to change. For two hundred years, during the reign of the Spanish colonists and after the liberation of the country by Simón Bolívar, only the daughters of families with grand names were permitted to enroll at the school that Fermina Daza attends. Now, things have changed. Fortunes have disappeared. A girl like

Fermina Daza is allowed to attend the prestigious school because her father has the money to pay for it, and some of the grand old families do not. The institutions of the city need new money from speculators, from foreigners moving to the city, and from mysterious men like Lorenzo Daza, who has no apparent source of income yet always pays in hard cash. Compromise is necessary.

Love and Cholera: The fear of cholera in the city is oppressive and pervasive, and it seems people have feared cholera forever. After finishing medical school in Paris, Dr. Urbino returned to the city in the wake of what is called "the great cholera epidemic." Throughout his life, he fends off illness by secretly medicating himself with pills. The centuries-old swamps within the city bubble with foul gasses, breed buzzard colonies, and host putrefying cholera bacteria born of flooded outdoor latrines. García Márquez suggests that lovesickness can be just as devastating as cholera. When love sickness infects Florentino Ariza, it gives him a high temperature, green vomit, and runny stool, the exact symptoms of cholera.

More Magic: Chapter 2 is rich in delightfully irrational details. Florentino Ariza's quadroon mother's poverty, dire despite the income from her notions shop and under-the-counter pawn shop, reduces her to tearing up old rags and selling them for bandages in order to feed her illegitimate child. Meanwhile, thin Florentino Ariza needs food so desperately that he holds on to every bit of sustenance in his body and suffers from chronic constipation. As a result of this malady of his youth, he will be forced to take enemas for the rest of his life. As a forlorn, large-eyed waif-child, Florentino Ariza meets the love of his life, Fermina Daza, in a house half in ruins. Fermina is reading to her illiterate aunt, a religious penitent who wears a habit. When Florentino Ariza hands Fermina Daza his first love letter, and bird droppings fall onto the white cloth, Florentino Ariza immediately assures her that the bird droppings symbolize good luck.

In a fantastical bit of medicine, Florentino Ariza's boss massages his minute sexual organs with a special snake venom ointment, a treatment so successful that it dazzles the local prostitutes. A sunken Spanish galleon lies at the bottom of the bay, just beyond the city, and Florentino Ariza dreams of salvaging its gold and giving it to Fermina Daza. Instead, he learns to play the violin and compose love melodies for her. Later, in his own little cubicle in the whorehouse, Florentino Ariza reads love verses and composes love letters for Fermina Daza, while naked young whores cavort about him, dressing, bathing, and feeding him bits of exotic foods. Compared to this richness, typical American fiction can seem anemic.

THE GOOD DOCTOR AND THE
CHOLERA DRAGON

Largely eradicated today, cholera still poses
a real health risk whenever earthquakes
and floods devastate a country. The disease
is caused by bacteria found in contaminated
water, which infests victims' intestines and
triggers bouts of diarrhea and immediate
dehydration. Death often occurs within
hours. In this novel, the stench of the bay,
which is mentioned frequently, likely results
from the same water contamination that
leads to cholera. Dr. Juvenal Urbino is his
city's St. George, and cholera is its dragon.

Chapter 3

The narrator tells us about Dr. Juvenal Urbino as he was at twenty-eight. After spending several years in Paris and receiving his degree in medicine, he comes home to Colombia fired with ambition and determined to cleanse his city of sewer filth and the rotting carcasses of dead animals. He plans to exterminate the thousands of rats and buzzards that infest the city. Like a self-anointed messiah of the city of his birth, Urbino will assemble a battalion of progressive-minded young men and establish a sanitized, thriving urban city, complete with European music, European literary traditions, and European rationality. Urbino's father, also a doctor, worked hard during the last cholera epidemic and ultimately died of the disease.

Miraculously, Urbino is not only a handsome bachelor, a fashionable dresser, and a terrific dancer, but a virgin. The local girls in the city hold lotteries, guessing which one of them he will choose, but he fools them all and chooses Fermina Daza, the daughter of a mule trader. However, obstinate Fermina has no intention of marrying Urbino.

Urbino first sees Fermina when Lorenzo Daza calls him in to examine her and to make sure she is not suffering from symptoms of cholera. Urbino examines Fermina Daza's naked breasts, lays his ear to her chest, and listens to her back. Never once during the examination does becomes sexually aroused. Only later does he remember her sky-blue chemise, feverish eyes, and long, dark hair.

Unlike his daughter, Lorenzo Daza is seduced by the grandeur of the young doctor—particularly his patrician name, Juvenal Urbino de la Calle. Passing the Daza residence later, Urbino sees Fermina painting. He interrupts her through an open window and asks to take her pulse. He declares that she is as healthy as a newly blossomed rose. Fermina Daza, silently vowing never to see him again, slams down the window. Lorenzo witnesses his daughter's effrontery and runs after Urbino, apologizing and begging Urbino to stay for coffee. After coffee, Urbino drinks several glasses of anisette and then launches into a pitch for Fermina Daza, saying she is fit to be the wife of a prince, despite her mulish character.

Upon reaching home, Urbino falls face down and then throws up. Soon afterward, he has a piano lifted onto a mule-driven wagon and hires a famous pianist to play a cycle of Mozart sonatas below Fermina Daza's window. Fermina looks out and wishes she had the courage to dump the contents of her chamber pot on Urbino and the pianist. Fermina Daza soon finds a richly monogrammed letter slipped under the front door. She burns it in her kerosene lamp.

Three more letters arrive, and then a little box of violet candies, and then a poison-pen letter and a black doll from Martinique. She is not intimidated.

Urbino convinces Sister Superior of the Blessed Virgin Academy to act as a go-between. The sister tells Fermina Daza that Urbino is a gift from Divine Providence. She offers Fermina Daza a gold and ivory rosary, which Fermina refuses. Sister Superior warns her that she can expect a visit from the Archbishop.

One day, Fermina and her cousin Hildebranda dress up like titled ladies of a long-gone era and parade through the streets to the studio of a Belgian photographer. When the girls emerge from the studio, catcalls and hostility greet them. Urbino swoops down in his carriage and carries them away to safety. Later, depressed that her father's mule-trading business has gone belly up and thinking about all the years she has yet to live, Fermina Daza decides to marry the young Doctor Urbino.

> "**M**ore important, with respect to García Márquez the writer, is an underlying lack of confidence in man's rational capacities…and his belief in the antirationalist tendency."
>
> **RAYMOND WILLIAMS**, *GABRIEL GARCÍA MÁRQUEZ*

She tells Florentino Ariza her plans. Left alone, he collapses in anguish. Uncle Leo XII, hoping to help his nephew, offers him a job as a telegraph operator in a far-away village in the Andes. To say farewell, Florentino Ariza stands under Fermina Daza's balcony with his violin and plays a love waltz that he composed for her. Then he boards a boat and begins his exile, watching bloated, green corpses float by. Gazing in silence at alligators sunning themselves and manatees nursing their young, he nurses his private grief. One night, however, a woman seizes his wrist and pulls him into a dark cabin. He loses his virginity to a naked woman smelling of salt and shrimp. Finished, she tells him to leave and to forget all about it.

Florentino Ariza tries to guess which of the women on board slept with him. He finally settles on **Rosalba**, but he never summons enough courage to speak to her. She soon disembarks along with two other women and a baby sleeping in a bird cage. Florentino tortures himself by imagining Fermina with Urbino. He vows to return to the city of Fermina Daza Urbino, where he will begin each day by dedicating himself to her.

Back home, Florentino Ariza offers shelter to Widow Nazaret, whose house is threatened by the civil war raging around them. She thanks him with feverish sex and then leaves his house to savor her rediscovery of the joys of sex. Florentino Ariza begins a new life, for after this, women see him as a man in need of love. Florentino begins recording his conquests in a chronicle he calls *Women*. Fifty years later, his twenty-five notebooks contain 622 coded entries.

The Urbinos return from a lengthy European honeymoon. Fermina Daza was not overly impressed with Europe. She is pregnant.

UNDERSTANDING AND INTERPRETING
Chapter 3

Two Desirable Men, One Handsome, One Shabby: No two people in this novel are more diametrically different from each other than Urbino and Florentino Ariza. The good-looking Urbino walks with a patrician air and has a medical degree from Paris. His goal is to lesson the threat of cholera in his city by ridding it of rats and sewer filth and by sanitizing its drinking water. He hopes to expose his fellow citizens to the joys of European music, art, and literature. In contrast, Florentino Ariza's single, supreme goal is to win the love of Fermina Daza and to marry her. His goal has nothing to do with the well-being of a city, and everything to do with himself and one woman.

Dressed in costly, immaculate suits, Urbino cuts a dashing figure next to Florentino Ariza, who always wears the same black hat, black bow tie, black coat, black pants, and black shoes, accessorized with a black umbrella. Urbino looks like a winner, and Florentino Ariza looks like a unkempt loser. And yet, we are told that the women of the city find the two men equally charming. In almost identical passages, García Márquez writes that local girls hold secret lotteries to guess who will spend time with Florentino Ariza and, later, with Urbino. The girls all lose. Both men choose the haughty, light-footed, almond-eyed Fermina Daza, a young girl with no social standing. For the moment, Florentino Ariza has lost Fermina Daza, but he is a patient man and plans to endure her marriage.

Ineffective but Heroic: Urbino's father, also a doctor, had his medical skills continually tested during the last cholera epidemic, and, ultimately, he fell victim to the plague he hoped to stop. At that time, scientific knowledge about cholera was still primitive. No known medication, drug, or remedy existed to stave off the ravages of the plague. Despite his best efforts, Urbino's father did almost nothing to help the multitude of dying victims. Even so, after the cholera epidemic subsided, he was honored as a hero for his unwavering diligence and self-sacrifice.

Fermina Succumbs: In Urbino and Ariza, Fermina has two vastly different suitors. In the last chapter, we saw Florentino Ariza's heartfelt entreaties, and now we observe Dr. Juvenal Urbino's excesses of courtship. Whatever Urbino's true

THE LITTLE TRAMP

In many of his films, Charlie Chaplin played a character called the Little Tramp, a nervous, slight man with a thick black moustache and enormous, romantic dark eyes. The Little Tramp always dressed in an ill-fitting black suit, black shoes, black bow tie, and black bowler hat. He also carried a black cane. In manner and dress, Florentino Ariza resembles the Little Tramp almost exactly. The only difference is that Chaplin leaned forward wistfully, two hands on his cane, whereas Florentino Ariza leans forward wistfully, two hands on his umbrella. Audiences adored Chaplin as the Little Tramp, much as we are instantly charmed by Florentino Ariza.

feelings for Fermina Daza, her persistent, arrogant rejection likely fuels his desire. Life has been easy for Urbino, and he is used to getting what he wants. Dumbfounded by Fermina's attitude, he hires a famous European pianist to serenade her with Mozart melodies. She ignores the gesture, just as she ignores a series of impressive letters, monogrammed and sealed with heavy wax. Even a poison pen letter and a doll do not sway her. Fermina's former teacher at the Academy cannot soften her resolve, even when she offers Fermina Daza a rare rosary and threatens a visit from the Archbishop himself.

When Fermina Daza finally agrees to marry Urbino, love has nothing to do with her decision. Her father, Lorenzo, has confessed that he is financially ruined. Shortly after this confession, Fermina Daza has a frightening nightmare about a paupers' cemetery. She spends a sleepless night thinking of all the many years she has yet to live. We also learn later that Fermina Daza is only a year from the official beginning of spinsterhood. Even though Fermina loathes herself for accepting her father's choice of a husband for her, she finally surrenders to Urbino's offer of marriage.

Surprised by Sex: Vaguely ready to take a vow of perpetual chastity in honor of his beloved Fermina Daza, Florentino Ariza ends up succumbing to sexual forces outside his control. Enduring the hardships of his journey upriver while watching choleric corpses float by, Florentino Ariza suffers from physical constipation, which suggests the pain of unrequited love. His self-imposed chastity comes to an abrupt end, however, when a sexually voracious woman ambushes him, yanks him into her dark cabin, and takes his virginity. This anonymous encounter sets into motion a long, picaresque series of sexual adventures. Florentino Ariza sleeps with hundreds of women, but, Don Quixote–like, he perpetually cherishes his version of Dulcinea: Fermina Daza.

Chapter 4

Florentino Ariza sees Fermina Daza in the atrium of the Cathedral, and she transfixes him. Her late pregnancy makes her elegant and beautiful. He knows that to win her he must accumulate fame and fortune, and Urbino must die. Florentino Ariza decides to become president of the R.C.C.—the River Company of the Caribbean—while he waits for Fermina.

Uncle Leo XII, current president of the company, initially shows reluctance to choose as his heir apparent thin, woeful-looking Florentino, who has not accomplished anything. Uncle Leo XII is a magician at making money, and a wonderful singer. His singing can flood funerals and make tombstones cry, but he wants to sing so sweetly that rare vases shatter. He agrees to let Florentino Ariza write bills of lading. Florentino Ariza fails miserably. He cannot write a single bill without turning it into a love poem. Sadly, Uncle Leo XII demotes him to the post of trash collector. Florentino Ariza succeeds at this and also begins a career writing love letters for the illiterate and the uninspired. He becomes very successful and learns to mimic handwriting, and soon he is answering the letters he wrote.

> "So far as this is Florentino's story, in a way his Bildüngsroman, we find ourselves, as he earns the suspension of our disbelief, cheering him on, wishing for the success of this stubborn warrior against age and death, and in the name of love. But like the best fictional characters, he insists on his autonomy, refusing to be anything less ambiguous than human."
>
> **THOMAS PYNCHON**

Florentino Ariza and his mother begin remodeling the family home in anticipation of Fermina's eventual arrival. Florentino Ariza's mother is mentally deteriorating. To escape the chaos of remodeling and the sadness of his mother's decline, Florentino Ariza begins having sex with women who live in the transient hotel. He becomes self-conscious about being seen with the same whores over and over, so he disguises them as men and takes them to bars. People see him taking these men to hotel rooms and conclude that Florentino Ariza is a sad-eyed homosexual.

A riverboat captain introduces Florentino Ariza to his mistress, the highly sexed, fifty-year-old Auscencia Santander, who takes a fancy to Florentino Ariza. When the captain is away, she walks around naked save a ribbon in her hair, and then she and Florentino Ariza have exhausting sex in the captain's bed. They fall fast asleep one afternoon after having sex and awaken to see that the captain walked in, saw them, and had everything moved out of the house except the bed and the lamps on the walls.

Florentino Ariza meets a flirtatious reveler during Carnival, a woman who turns out to be an escaped inmate from the insane asylum. The woman beheaded a guard and wounded two others with a machete. Florentino Ariza is heartbroken when she is led away. On Ash Wednesday, he begins standing outside the asylum, trying to get English chocolates to his beloved. One day, Florentino Ariza meets **Leona Cassiani**, a sexy, dark-eyed black woman. They soon begin meeting for sex, and he convinces Uncle Leo XII to offer her a menial job in his company. Before long, Leona Cassiani so impresses Uncle Leo XII that he makes her his executive secretary.

Years pass. One day, Dr. Urbino comes to Florentino Ariza's R.C.C. office. He gasps that a cyclone is coming, but he will wait to speak to Uncle Leo XII despite it. He and Florentino Ariza speak tensely about music and the declining state of the arts. Urbino says he is considering reviving the Poetic Festival, which makes Florentino Ariza ecstatic.

The Poetic Festival is revived and Florentino Ariza enters, convinced he will win. Fermina Daza announces the winner, a peculiar Chinese man who kisses the Golden Orchid trophy while thousands of Colombians jeer. Afterward, all Florentino Ariza remembers only the plump woman beside him who comforted him when she saw the flower on his lap wilt as Fermina Daza announced the winner. The woman, **Sara Noriega**, takes Florentino Ariza to her home. She sucks on a baby's pacifier, and Florentino Ariza fends off attacks from her jealous cat. They have a five-year affair, but one day Sara ends it and they never see each other again. Sara tells Florentino Ariza she thinks Fermina Daza's marriage to Urbino is loveless.

In a sense, Sara is right. Urbino and Fermina Daza did not love each other when they married. Fermina Daza hated the idea of the marriage, but she was twenty-one, and Urbino could give her security. She soon gave birth to a son, but even her pleasure in the child could not block out her mother-in-law's continual complaining about Fermina Daza's clothes and table manners. Fermina Daza discovers one day that her favorite food is mashed, seasoned eggplant, the one food she made young Florentino Ariza swear never to force her to eat. Appalled at her metamorphosis, she demands to move to Europe. Urbino obliges her.

Florentino Ariza begins entertaining himself by writing tiny love letters and attaching them to the legs of a homing pigeon belonging to a woman named Olimpia Zuleta. Florentino and Olimpia sleep together. One afternoon, Florentino Ariza dips a finger into a can of red paint and writes above Olimpia's crotch that it belongs to him. Olimpia undresses before her husband that night, and he sees the boast and slashes Olimpia's throat with a razor.

Years pass. Fermina Daza's son goes to medical school, and she has a daughter, Ofelia. She and Urbino return from Europe, and Fermina Daza realizes that she has become a servant to her demanding husband. She learns of Florentino Ariza's professional success in the R.C.C. and she is pleased. Fermina Daza does love Urbino after being with him for thirty years. They have become a single, if divided, being.

UNDERSTANDING AND INTERPRETING

Chapter 4

Florentino Ariza's Mentors: Florentino Ariza has several mentors who serve as teachers and guides during the course of this novel. Uncle Leo XII, though at first hesitant to take on his melancholy nephew, is instrumental in setting Florentino Ariza on the path to becoming president of the River Company of the Caribbean. Uncle Leo XII also provides a living object lesson for his nephew, stubbornly pursuing his dreams in the face of difficulties. García Márquez calls this curly-headed, faun-lipped man a "genial lunatic," for above everything else, even more than he loves making money, Uncle Leo XII loves to sing. His single goal is to sing so skillfully that can shatter rare vases. He never succeeds, but he never gives up on this dream. His lovely singing always breaks the hearts of his listeners. Florentino Ariza's poetic, lyrical excesses seem to have genetic origins in his uncle.

> "I don't know who said that novelists read the novels of others only to figure out how they are written. I believe it's true. We aren't satisfied with the secrets exposed on the surface of the page: we turn the book around to find the seams."
>
> **GABRIEL GARCÍA MÁRQUEZ**

Uncle Leo XII's music teacher also mentors Florentino Ariza. He secures a tiny cubicle in the local whorehouse for Florentino Ariza so that Florentino Ariza has a place to scribble impassioned love lyrics and read classic romantic novels along with the latest romantic ones. The music teacher immediately recognizes that Florentino Ariza has an all-consuming need for love. It is the music teacher who convinces Uncle Leo XII to hire Florentino to write bills of lading, a kind gesture even though Florentino Ariza bungles the job by turning the bills into verses about everlasting love. The music teacher has successfully trained Florentino Ariza as a telegraph assistant, and Florentino Ariza uses that knowledge to network with outlying telegraph operators and keep track of Fermina Daza's odyssey with her father.

Leona Cassiani, another mentor, appears in Florentino Ariza's life by chance one day. For a long time, Florentino regrets his decision not to have sex with Leona, a decision he made because he thought he would have to pay her for sex, and paying for sex is against his principles. Like Florentino, Leona Cassiani is an unlikely success story. This pretty woman, bespangled with clanking earrings and noisy bracelets, begins working in a menial position for the R.C.C. and eventually becomes executive secretary to Uncle Leo XII. Seeing the example of Leona's achievement further steels Florentino Ariza's resolve to renew his vow of eternal love for Fermina Daza and eventually marry her.

Sara Noriega, another mentor who Florentino Ariza meets by chance, intuitively sympathizes with his misery. She sees how it devastates him to hear the love of his life, Fermina Daza, read not his name as the winner of the Poetic Festival award, but the name of another man. Sara cares so much for Florentino Ariza that she declaws her pet cat so that it can no longer attack and shred Florentino Ariza's back when Sara and Florentino Ariza are having sex. Sara's understanding of the poetic vocation makes it easy for Florentino Ariza to adore her, although he always behaves as if he is the husband of Fermina Daza. Sara gives Florentino Ariza wise counsel, telling him that spiritual love exists from the waist up, and physical love exists from the waist down. She insists that Fermina Daza did not love Urbino when she married him, an opinion that delights Florentino Ariza.

Melancholy Humor: There are several instances of rueful humor in this chapter. Florentino Ariza writes a highly poetic, long-winded, multi-volume *Lovers' Companion* that describes every possible situation that he and Fermina Daza might find themselves in that would require love letters. When Florentino Ariza makes plans to publish the book, however, no printer will touch it. Love letters have gone out of fashion. Later, when Florentino Ariza falls victim to a fascinating, long-haired, mysterious beauty during Carnival, they dance wildly, reveling like new sweethearts. She laughingly warns him that she is crazy. She seems to be joking, but it turns out that she truly is clinically insane. She has escaped from the local asylum after decapitating a guard and wounding two others with a machete.

Chapter 5

On the first morning of the twentieth century, an enormous, multicolored hot air balloon slowly ascends above the seacoast city. Among the dignitaries aboard are the illustrious doctor and progressive civic leader Juvenal Urbino and his lovely wife, Fermina Daza. They carry the first piece of airmail to San Juan de la Ciénaga, about ninety miles north. Florentino Ariza's progress up the managerial ladder of the R.C.C. means he is now invited to such events, and he watches the balloon rise. One day, Florentino Ariza realizes that Fermina Daza, usually a constant public figure, has disappeared. Rumor has it she has fled the city by night

LONGER THAN SORROW

When Florentino Ariza, Urbino, and Fermina Daza go to the movies, they see *Cabiria*, a groundbreaking spectacle of the silent film era. The film's plot focuses on a young Roman virgin separated from her parents and thrust into a salacious Roman arena of sex and the worship of the pagan god Moloch. The historical epic was released in 1914. It featured lavish costumes, gigantic sets, and special effects, and had a running time of 123 minutes, a record-breaking length in those days and reason enough for Fermina Daza to gasp that the film seems "longer than sorrow."

and is now dying of consumption. However, Fermina Daza is perfectly healthy. For two years, she has been living with her cousin Hildebranda Sánchez.

Fermina Daza fled for a particular reason. By habit, she smells the clothes that her family takes off every night. One day, she smelled a strange odor and realized that Urbino was having sex with another woman. Urbino became evasive and short-tempered. One day, Fermina Daza asked him what was happening, and Urbino told her everything. One day he had seen Miss Barbara Lynch, a blazingly beautiful mixed-race woman in a white polka-dotted red dress, become obsessed, and started an affair with her.

Urbino was distressed to realize that Barbara's bedroom window overlooked a schoolroom of children. To speed up the process, Barbara scheduled quick trysts only during afternoon recess and wore no underwear. The coachman suspected Urbino's infidelity, as did most of Barbara's neighbors. Finally, Urbino felt so guilty that he went to confession and vowed to stop seeing Miss Lynch.

Urbino expects Fermina Daza to be understanding when he returns and asks for her forgiveness. Fermina Daza grows wrinkled and pale, convinced that people are laughing at her. Her anger overflows, and her tears run down her cheeks and burn her nightgown. What angers Fermina Daza most is that Urbino confessed every detail of his infidelity to a man, a priest. Fermina Daza thinks no one gossips more than priests. A few days later, she boards a boat and goes to her mother's relatives. Two years later, Urbino arrives at Hildebranda's ranch and discovers that Fermina Daza's anger has dissipated, and she wants to go home.

One night in the cinema, Florentino Ariza hears Fermina Daza's husky, unmistakable voice commenting on the extraordinary length of the movie: "My God, this is longer than sorrow." Florentino Ariza is jubilant.

The film ends, and Florentino Ariza and Leona Cassiani suddenly come face to face with Fermina Daza and Urbino. They exchange courtesies, and Florentino Ariza is thunderstruck at Fermina Daza's beauty. As Fermina Daza leaves the movie theater, Florentino Ariza sees her stumble and almost fall. Age, not consumption, has secretly compromised her body. Florentino Ariza himself greatly fears aging. He refuses to become an old, shuffling man.

Florentino Ariza thinks that sex with Leona might soothe him, but she brushes him aside and says she realized a long time ago that he was not the man she was looking for. Later, Florentino Ariza thinks more about aging. He has lost all his hair, despite more than 172 valiant attempts to save a few remaining sprigs. His teeth have all been pulled by an itinerant dentist cheered on by Uncle Leo XII, who takes an obsessive interest in false teeth.

Uncle Leo XII genuinely likes his nephew and is particularly pleased when he accidentally walks in on Florentino Ariza having sex. This disproves the rumors

HORNS OF CUCKOLDRY

Lost in reverie, remembering the many women with whom he has had sex, Florentino Ariza thinks of those who sleep beside their husbands, "their horns golden in the moonlight." The mention of horns is an allusion to the mythological horns that sprout from the heads of men whose wives are unfaithful to them. These men, cuckolds, are often jeeringly called "unicorns," especially in Italy, Spain, and Latin America.

that Florentino Ariza is a homosexual, and thus Uncle Leo XII begins to seriously consider him as an heir. All of Leo's sons have died, and all of his daughters have moved to New York. Six months later, Florentino Ariza is named President of the R.C.C.

Florentino Ariza reflects on the women who have helped him fend off boredom, thinking of those now in their graves and those now asleep with their husbands, men whose "horns [are] golden in the moonlight." He thinks of the mysterious Rosalba, to whom he lost his virginity, and of the Widow Nazaret, his lover for almost thirty years. He thinks of the nude cellist, the threatening gardening shears of another widow, the woman who ripped all the buttons from his clothes, and many, many more. He sighs, realizing that his heart "contains more rooms than a whorehouse."

Florentino Ariza has been sleeping with his ward, a long-braided nymphet named América Vicuña. He is lying in her arms when he hears the Cathedral bells tolling repeatedly, the signal that an important person has died. When Florentino Ariza discovers that Dr. Juvenal Urbino is the dead man, terror seizes him. Now he must talk to Fermina Daza, to whom he has never been emotionally disloyal. Florentino Ariza goes to the Urbino mansion and repeats his vow of eternal fidelity and everlasting love to Fermina Daza. Although crushed by her rejection, he refuses to renounce hope. After two weeks, he discovers a letter floating in a puddle in his courtyard. He recognizes the handwriting on it.

UNDERSTANDING AND INTERPRETING

Chapter 5

Odors, Delicious and Rank: Smelling and sniffing, foul odors and pleasant fragrances permeate this novel. Fermina Daza's longtime habit of smelling her family's discarded clothes is only the latest entry in a long line of smelling stories. The novel opens with the scent of bitter almonds, olfactory evidence that Jeremiah died from inhaling the fumes of gold cyanide. Urbino keeps a pad of camphor in his suit pocket to inhale whenever he feels anxious. On the way to seek out Jeremiah's secret lover, the stench of suffocating gases in her neighborhood sickens Urbino, as does the putrid quagmire of the slaughterhouse in the streets. The ever-present reek of rotting animals and human waste lies in the bay, just beyond the city. Urbino delights in the smell of his own urine after devouring his fill of fresh asparagus. Being a doctor, Urbino is aware of the specific, unmistakable odors of many things—old age, for example, with its sour perspiration and stale breath.

Gabriel García Márquez

The young Florentino Ariza usually surrounds himself with fragrant aromas. He wears a camellia in his lapel when he begins courting Fermina Daza. Standing next to her, he notices a floral perfume from her gardenia garland, a smell he identifies with her for the rest of his life. When Fermina Daza and her father trek along the rim of the Andes, their urine-stained cots disgust her. Returning home from her long visit with relatives, Fermina Daza visits the local market and deeply inhales the scent of the open, pungent barrels of pickled herring. She crushes sage leaves and oregano in her palms and breathes in their fragrances, delighting in the anise and ginger root and the perfume from Paris. On his own lonely journey away from the city, Florentino Ariza loses his virginity to an anonymous woman who smells of salt and shrimp. And later, after Fermina Daza and Urbino have been married for a very long time, their long-lasting spat concerns soap, which is used to wash away odors. Urbino, Florentino Ariza, and Fermina Daza are all sharply sensitive to smells, and it is no surprise that Fermina Daza ferrets out the secrets of her husband's sex life just by smelling his clothes.

Sex in the Time of Cholera: "Choler," a medieval word for anger, aptly describes Fermina Daza's reaction to Urbino's infatuation with Miss Barbara Lynch. Fermina Daza's deepest assumptions have been shaken, and she becomes scared and furious. When Fermina Daza married Urbino, she did not love him and he did not love her. After years of living together, however, they have become like two halves of the same being. A quiet sort of love, encompassing boredom, familiarity, and affection, has knitted what Fermina Daza believes is an everlasting bond of fidelity between her and Urbino. He is her bastion against such emotional hurricanes as Florentino Ariza's nonstop declarations of love and against unexpected poverty, which she suffered with her father. Both Florentino Ariza and Lorenzo Daza were unpredictable, emotionally open men. Fermina Daza chose to marry the rational Urbino, who vowed to scientifically rid his city of cholera and systematically install a new sewer system. He epitomizes progress, even traveling in the hot air balloon that delivers the city's first piece of air mail correspondence.

This scientist, this man of calm, prudence, objectivity, and stability, is the very last person Fermina Daza would imagine capable of straying from the marital bed. When Urbino confesses his infidelity, Fermina Daza's smoothly running world jumps its track. Her importance to Urbino suddenly seems uncertain. Her role in his life is ill-defined. She weeps, rages, and wishes Urbino were dead. Her face wrinkles, her lips pale, and her hair looks lifeless. She becomes convinced that people laugh and gossip about her, so she leaves the city for two years. On the surface, Fermina Daza might seem jealous, but she is not. She knows that Miss Barbara Lynch has not replaced her in Urbino's heart. Fermina Daza is enraged that her expectations have been ignored, humiliated that her husband has been acting like a randy old goat, and disgusted that he has confessed his sins to a priest out of a weak desire to be forgiven and made to feel better.

Urbino seems infected by a last-ditch desire to prove to himself that his sexuality is still potent. For years, Urbino has lived in a prison of his own making, trapping himself in routines. His affair with Barbara Lynch is his sexual jailbreak. Urbino expects nothing less than understanding from Fermina Daza when he returns and asks for forgiveness. Fermina Daza does not react with understanding, however, but with bitter anger. García Márquez emphasizes her anger by making her tears burn her nightgown. Urbino feels sure that eventually his wife's rage will abate, but as she leaves him, Fermina Daza is determined that her rage will burn forever.

Chapter 6

Widowhood does not become Fermina Daza. She is angry with Urbino for deserting her and angry with Florentino Ariza for being impertinent. Her three-page letter to Florentino Ariza expresses her rage. She begins burning treasures that she and Urbino collected abroad and adds to the pyre every piece of clothing and furniture that reminds her of Urbino. Despite this burning, the wasted years she spent in servitude haunt her.

Florentino Ariza, meanwhile, makes plans to marry Fermina Daza and begins remodeling his house. He writes letters to her that are not lyrical and romantic, but philosophical. These letters calm Fermina Daza. She allows Florentino Ariza to begin visiting her, asking him questions about the riverboats that his company owns. They both agree that river travel is preferable to flying, since airplanes are "flying coffins." Florentino Ariza's visits become regular, and he begins surprising Fermina Daza with small gifts of English biscuits, Greek olives, and other delicacies. When Florentino Ariza is injured for a while and cannot visit, Fermina realizes she misses his company.

Fermina Daza's son tries and fails to discourage his mother's friendship with Florentino Ariza. Ofelia, Fermina Daza's daughter, rushes down from New Orleans and badmouths Florentino Ariza, so infuriating Fermina Daza that she orders Ofelia out of the house. A series of front-page stories run in a local paper supposedly exposing Urbino as an adulterer and Fermina Daza's father as the

YOU AND YOU

When Florentino Ariza begins courting Fermina Daza again, he reminds her that they used to use the *tu* form of address instead of the more formal *usted*. In Spanish, "usted," which means "you," is used when talking to colleagues, new acquaintances, or elders. It shows respect. "Tu," which also means "you," is used when speaking to children, family members, and close friends. The old-fashioned English equivalent of "tu" is "thou," an affectionate address rarely used today except in love poetry or religious literature. The switch from the formal "you" to the familiar "you" would have been a happy moment for the young Florentino Ariza, because it indicated his affectionate, familiar relationship with Fermina Daza.

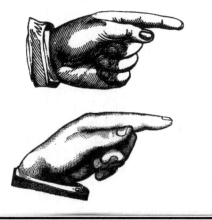

mastermind of a counterfeiting ring. When Fermina Daza reads an anonymously published defense of her family, she rallies: the style is unmistakably Florentino Ariza's. She invites him to visit her, and when he does, he suggests that Fermina Daza might enjoy a pleasure cruise down the river in one of his ships. She readily agrees.

Fermina Daza's son accompanies her to the *New Fidelity* and is impressed by his mother's luxurious presidential suite and by the captain's gift of smoked salmon and champagne. He does not suspect that Florentino Ariza, President of the R.C.C., provided these luxuries, and only learns at the last minute that Florentino Ariza will sail with his mother. As the ship sails out of the bay, Fermina Daza indulges in her secret vice, cigarettes. She rolls her own and smokes them nonstop. Florentino Ariza savors *his* secret vice, rich mountain coffee. They tentatively hold hands. Florentino Ariza leans forward for a kiss, but Fermina Daza refuses, fearing that she might "smell like an old woman." The next morning, she discovers a single white rose in a vase on her night table. As if in a vision, Fermina Daza sees Urbino on a passing boat, tipping his hat to her, "his official love," bidding her farewell. That night, she asks God to please let the awkward, lovesick Florentino know how to begin the next day.

The next morning, she dons a simple gray dress, and on deck she discovers that Florentino Ariza has emerged from his cocoon in fashionable clothes and sunglasses. As the ship slowly sails up the river, Fermina Daza and Florentino Ariza realize that they have begun to act like young sweethearts. Florentino Ariza rolls cigarettes for Fermina Daza, and they laugh about old times. Florentino Ariza again attempts a kiss. Trembling, Fermina Daza obliges, sighing that ships make her crazy.

> "There is nothing I have read quite like this astonishing final chapter, symphonic, sure in its dynamics and tempo, moving like a riverboat too, its author and pilot, with a lifetime's experience steering us unerringly among hazards of skepticism and mercy, on this river we all know, without whose navigation there is no love and against whose flow the effort to return is never worth a less honorable name than remembrance."
>
> **THOMAS PYNCHON**

When the *New Fidelity* runs out of oil and is stranded for almost a week, Florentino Ariza and Fermina Daza see a perfect opportunity to have sex. Fermina Daza wants nothing fast and furtive. She wants to "do it like grownups." Florentino Ariza is impotent the first time they try, but the next day he undresses dramatically and displays his erection as it is a war trophy. Fermina Daza feels unnerved afterward, for she had not had sex in nearly twenty years. By the time the ship reaches La Dorada, she and Florentino Ariza seem like enchanted lovers, showered with daily fresh roses from the captain, serenaded with old waltzes, and served dainty morsels secretly laced with aphrodisiacs.

In order to sustain this intoxicating happiness, Florentino Ariza speaks to the captain, and they devise a plan. The ship will unload its cargo and its passengers, and the captain will hoist a yellow flag, signaling that there is cholera on board. Only Florentino Ariza, Fermina Daza, and the captain and his masculine lady friend will make the return trip. On the first night under the cholera flag, Fermina Daza descends to the ship's kitchen and creates an extraordinary casserole, which Florentino Ariza christens "Eggplant al Amour."

The trip homeward is punctuated by cannon shots, fired heavenward by superstitious villagers along the river in order to frighten away the cholera. Florentino Ariza plays waltzes for Fermina Daza on a violin, the captain and his lady dance, and at last they near port. They do not like the landscape they see as they sail up the Magdalena River. The forests are destroyed, and the alligators and manatees are gone. Fermina Daza dreads leaving the ship, and the port authorities do not welcome passengers from a cholera ship.

Florentino Ariza shouts to the captain that they should return to La Dorada, and once they reach La Dorada, they should turn around and sail back here, then reverse course and sail again toward La Dorada. The captain hears these orders in disbelief. He asks how long he is supposed to continue this coming and going. "Forever," answers Florentino Ariza.

UNDERSTANDING AND INTERPRETING
Chapter 6

The New and Improved Fermina Daza: For over fifty years, Fermina Daza has been a wife and a mother, and now a grandmother. Mostly, she has been a wife, an appendage of her illustrious husband. Her role has been strictly defined during her marriage to Urbino. She has maintained a strict scheduling of her own life in order to help her husband maintain his own precise scheduling. When Urbino dies suddenly, it enrages Fermina Daza. She structured her life around him, and now she is left without a role to play or a sense of who she is. She feels like a ghost in a strange house. Like the Amazon queen Dido in Virgil's *Aeneid*, whose beloved Aeneas suddenly leaves after vowing to stay forever, Fermina Daza prepares an enormous pyre. Onto this pyre she tosses all of Urbino's "armor"—his expensive clothes, shoes, hats, even his rocking chair—and sets fire to it. The bonfire is volcanic.

However, Urbino is not so easily destroyed. His scent remains, and memories of him remain. Total eradication seems impossible, and thus Fermina Daza takes a new tack and begins to eradicate her old, role-playing self. She slowly becomes a new woman, one who allows herself to take comfort in Florentino Ariza's new stream of meditative letters. These philosophical, calming letters help her recover her peace of mind. Months pass, and when Florentino Ariza comes to call, she receives him, finally acknowledging him. For weeks, they share old memories and speak of the ships that sail for his company, and he begins to bring her small gifts and roses. When Fermina Daza is emotionally undone by slanderous stories in the newspaper about her late husband and her father, it is Florentino Ariza who publishes a letter of defense, signed with a pseudonym. Fermina Daza begins to rely on Florentino Ariza and to feel deeply grateful to him. She defies her censorious son and daughter and joyfully accepts Florentino's suggestion that they get away from the fetid swamp of old memories and make new memories. Not only does she welcome the invitation, she confides to him that she would like to keep going and going and never to come back.

Onboard the *New Fidelity*, Fermina Daza blossoms into a cigarette-smoking, vivacious, inviting, sexual woman. When she and Florentino sit alone on deck, he timidly reaches a hand toward her and discovers that hers is waiting for him. For the first time in over fifty years, Fermina Daza feels absolutely free—free of years of misunderstandings, useless arguments, and unresolved angers.

The Metamorphosis of Florentino Ariza: Florentino Ariza's change of clothes symbolizes his change of spirits. After more than fifty years, Florentino Ariza sheds his misshapen black suit, black shoes, and black bow tie like the husk of a dying insect and emerges next morning on deck, dressed all in white, wearing a rakish white cap and sunglasses. He is a man reborn, his vow of love still unblemished and pure and as snow white as his clothing. The name of the ship, the *New Fidelity*, perfectly captures the spirit of the new romance between Fermina Daza and Florentino Ariza.

Florentino Ariza has come out of exile. Fermina is his, and he belongs to Fermina. When they make love, he sees her wrinkled shoulders, sagging breasts, and flabby skin, but he still finds her beautiful. He loves her as passionately and as spiritually as he did when they were teenagers. His love for

Fermina transcends the physical changes that have reshaped her body. Despite Florentino Ariza's hundreds of sexual adventures, this one is the grand adventure, the one he has anticipated for more than fifty years. Florentino Ariza and Fermina Daza have survived, and their love for one another has survived. They have even survived the cholera plague and harnessed it to work for them. When the captain hoists the yellow flag of cholera so that they can be alone, sailing back and forth on the river, the cholera flag changes from a terrifying symbol of death to an irreverent, sneaky means of enjoying sex and love.

Conclusions

Florentino Ariza's seemingly absurd vow to wait for Fermina Daza until Urbino dies actually proves sensible. Still, the fifty-plus years of waiting try the health and patience of both Florentino Ariza and Fermina Daza. The half-century is one of threatening civil wars, storms and cyclones, the plague of cholera, and the deaths of beloved people in both of their lives. These dramatic and sad episodes run alongside the fantastical, consistent love-in-limbo of Florentino Ariza for Fermina Daza.

Florentino Ariza manages to wait fifty years for Fermina Daza partly by reveling in his memories of her. Because he must satisfy his physical longings, Florentino Ariza makes love to women—but his sexual relationships with women go far beyond satisfying longings. Because he never flags in his emotional devotion to Fermina Daza, Florentino Ariza can have sex without becoming emotionally entangled with his partners. Sex for him is art, companionship, an expression of affection, but nothing to do with the love he feels for Fermina Daza. As Sara Noriega, one of his sexual partners, tells him, "Spiritual love [is] from the waist up and physical love [is] from the waist down." Florentino Ariza loves Fermina Daza from the waist up. His love for her is like Dante's love for Beatrice and Petrarch's love for Laura. Florentino Ariza considers himself a virgin despite his more than six hundred sexual encounters with women, because until he sleeps with Fermina Daza, he has not slept with the woman he loves.

SUGGESTIONS
FOR FURTHER
READING

Alvarez-Borland, Isabel. "From Mystery to Parody: (Re)Readings of García Márquez's *Chronicle of a Death Foretold.*" *Modern Critical Views.* New York: Chelsea House Publishers, 1989.

Bell, Michael. *Gabriel García Márquez: Solitude and Solidarity.* New York: St. Martin's Press, 1993.

Bell-Villada, Gene. *García Márquez: The Man and His Work.* Chapel Hill: University of North Carolina Press, 1990.

Dolan, Sean. *Gabriel García Márquez.* New York: Chelsea House, 1994.

Hamill, Pete. "Love and Solitude." *Vanity Fair,* March 1998. 124–131, 191–192.

Harss, Luis, and Barbara Dohmann. *Into the Mainstream: Conversations with Latin-American Writers.* New York: Harper, 1967.

Janes, Regina. One Hundred Years of Solitude: *Modes of Reading.* New York: Macmillan, 1991.

Llosa, Mario Vargas. "Gabriel García Márquez: From Aracataca to Macondo." *Modern Critical Views: Gabriel García Márquez.* New York: Chelsea House Publishers, 1989.

McGuirk, Bernard, and Richard Cardwell, eds. *Gabriel García Márquez: New Readings.* New York: Cambridge University Press, 1988.

McMurray, George R., ed. *Critical Essays on Gabriel García Márquez.* New York: Macmillan, 1987.

McNerney, Kathleen. *Understanding Gabriel García Márquez.* Columbia: University of South Carolina Press, 1989.

Palencia-Roth, Michael. *Myth and the Modern Novel: García Márquez, Mann, and Joyce.* New York: Garland, 1987.

Pritchett, V.S. *The Myth Makers.* New York: Random House, 1979.

Williams, Raymond L. *Gabriel García Márquez.* New York: Twayne, 1984.

INDEX